# Drinking & Driving

## Know Your Limits and Liabilities

Marshall B. Stearn, Ph.D.

Park West Publishing Co.
Sausalito, California
1985

© 1985   Marshall B. Stearn, Ph.D.

Published by                363.1
Park West Publishing Co.        S
Post Office Box 1502
Sausalito, California 94920

The California Highway Patrol granted permission to reprint the anti-drinking and driving logo for the cover.

For information contact: Park West Publishing Co.

Printed in the United States of America
ISBN 0-9610480-2-6

# Dedication

*To David and Heidi*

# Table of Contents

# Foreword

The profound negative affect that alcohol has had on my immediate family inspired the research and publication of this book.

The national ethics of drinking, as a way of life, are difficult to change. Even on an individual level a person's consciousness often must be significantly jolted in order to internalize the problem and attempt to change. This jolt may come about in many ways, but the most effective instrument of change is experiencing a real need, whether physical or spiritual, to make the effort to bring about lasting change. Of course an unexpected tragedy is, in many cases, the reason why a person's behavior will change.

The drinking and driving epidemic which now plagues the United States is also a global disaster. Hopefully, the data gathered here will have an impact on the general public.

I wish to thank the many people and agencies who lent their advice, encouragement, and support to this project.

Marshall B. Stearn, Ph.D.

# Acknowledgements

Sincere thanks to David Bessie, Quentin Durham, Barbara Hanchette, Brian Kuester, Jay Oliver, Kim Peterson, Carol Shinefield, and Tonia Sedlock for their technical help and assistance.

Special thanks to Alcoholics Anonymous, Allstate Insurance Company, California Highway Partol, National Council on Alcohol, National Highway Traffic Safety Council, MADD, RID, SADD, and the United States Department of Health and Human Resources for their help and assistance.

# Introduction

Alcohol is a major contributing factor in automobile crashes, Approximately sixty percent of fatal crashes each year involve a driver who had been drinking. In fact, more than three-quarters of these drivers had a blood alcohol level that exceeded the .10 percent limit required for presumed intoxication; on the average their blood alcohol content (BAC) was found to be .20 percent. According to the National Council on Alcoholism, of the people stopped for driving under the influence (DUI) and cited for drunk driving, two-thirds are deemed to have a drinking problem.

To gain some perspective on the gravity and horror that are the results of drinking and driving, consider the following scenario:

Madigan Army Hospital in Tacoma, Washington prepared a Memorial Day weekend safety campaign by demonstrating the effects of a high-speed auto crash. A car traveling at fifty-five miles per hour and containing a test-mannequin, crashed into a tree. Using time-lapse photography, the following results were demonstrated.[1]

**1/10 of a second:**
The front bumper and chrome frosting of the grillwork collapse. Slivers of steel penetrate the tree to a depth of over one inch.

**2/10 of a second:**
The hood crumples and smashes into the windshield.

13

Spinning rear wheels leave the ground. As the fenders come into contact with the tree, the car bends in the middle with the rear end bucking over the front end of the car.

### 3/10 of a second:

The mannequin's body is now off the seat, torso upright, knees pressing against the dashboard. The plastic and steel frame of the steering wheel begins to bend under the weight of the mannequin. Its head is near the sun visor, the chest above the steering column.

### 4/10 of a second:

The car's front twenty-four inches have been demolished, but the rear end is still traveling at an estimated thirty-five miles per hour, and the mannequin is still traveling at fifty-five miles per hour. The half-ton engine block crunches into the tree. The rear end of the car, still bucking like a horse, rises high enough to scrape bark off low branches.

### 5/10 of a second:

The mannequin's hands, frozen onto the steering wheel, bend the steering column into an almost vertical position. The force of gravity then pushes him into the steering column.

### 6/10 of a second:

The brake pedal shears off at the floor boards. The chassis bends in the middle, shearing body bolts. The rear of the car begins to fall back down; its spinning wheels dig into the ground.

### 7/10 of a second:

The seat of the car rams forward, pinning the mannequin against the steering shaft; the hinges tear, and the doors spring open.

Given this scenario, it takes little imagination to project what would happen to a human driver or passenger. It is clear that driver skills, at best, have to be in top form simply to respond to an emergency. When alcohol or other chemicals are affecting the driver, the chances of making the correct judgment or move to avoid a tragic event grow even slimmer.

25,000 individuals die each year in automobile crashes involving alcohol and/or drug use. One authority in the field has stated that, "Death on the highway is a socially acceptable way to commit murder." Every holiday season is haunted by the perplexing problem of the drinking driver, and law enforcement crackdowns do not adequately deal with this problem. Some experts from the California Highway Patrol suggest that current laws are not being enforced with enough vigor, while others complain that there are too many loopholes for drunk drivers to slip through. Courts in some counties have even allowed drunk drivers to plead guilty to lesser charges in order to avoid jury trials.

The real problem lies in the fact that our society still condones drunk driving. An example of our tolerant attitude toward drinking and driving is illustrated in this quote from the *Los Angeles Times.*

> Cesar Cedeno was in for a lot of ribbing after returning from Houston where he pleaded no contest to a charge of intoxication and running his car into a tree. He had to pay $7,000 in property damage. Said Dave Parker of the Cincinatti Reds, "If I'd paid $7,000 for a tree I'd have at least gotten the firewood for my fireplace."[2]

This cavalier attitude, used by the print media to highlight a potentially grievous event, is the type of mentality that contributes to and perpetuates the idea that drinking and getting drunk are good fun. As two judges in Napa, California put it, "The heart of the drunk driving problem lies in the habits of our society. Action must be taken to change those habits."[3] And a recent editorial in the *San Francisco Chronicle* stated, "The drunk driving problem will be resolved only when the public views it as criminal conduct."[4] This editorial also stated that the long-range answer to this problem lies in reshaping the way society views drunk driving. If drunk driving continues to be accepted with a "boys will be boys" attitude, it will remain a major problem and a major killer.

Another frequently encountered problem is that of consistency in the courts. Drunk drivers cannot simply be dismissed from the courtroom with a slap on the wrist because the judges are afraid of court backlogs. An editorial from the *San Francisco Chronicle* goes so far as to suggest, "If the government takes planes and boats away from drug dealers, why not take the car away from a convicted drunk driver?" However, according to Dan Parker of the California Highway Patrol, "There are too many loopholes; a person can get around the law if they really try. I don't think there's a panacea, inhibiting drinking and driving, the real answer is getting people to change their behavior."[5]

In this book I have tried to emphasize the effects of alcohol on the body and organ systems and how it impairs the skills necessary to handle a motor vehicle safely and competently. In addition I have provided some resources for communities seeking help with drinking drivers, and for individuals with behavior problems related to alcohol who need assistance. I have also included the current DUI laws for each state which inform people of their limits and liabilities related to being arrested for *driving under the influence.*

# Chapter 1

---

# Drinking, Driving, and Drugs

Alcohol is a mind-altering drug that works as a sedative; it changes the way a person thinks and acts. It affects judgment and coordination, and is a factor in sixty percent of American highway deaths.

The 1982 Gallup Poll reported that one out of every three families claimed alcohol had adversely affected their family life. Moreover, less than seven percent of this alcoholic population is of the skid-row type which means that ninety-three percent of the alcoholic population are what professionals in the field call "functional alcoholics."[6] Furthermore, millions of people take drugs everyday, often unaware that these substances can affect their driving skills. Tranquilizers, marijuana, and a variety of other drugs, including some over-the-counter medicines, can affect the mental and physical skills needed for safe driving. The effects of a drug vary significantly from one individual to the next, and can even vary in the same individual at different times. The driver's age, sex, weight, and emotional state; the dosage; and when the drug was taken are all factors which can influence the effects of a drug on a person's ability to drive safely.

Taking more than one drug at a time is especially dangerous because each drug can aggravate the impact of the other. This is particularly true when one of the drugs is alcohol. It is well known that alcohol increases the sedative effect of tranquilizers and barbiturates (sleeping pills). Other substances may be hazardous combinations due to popular misconceptions about their properties. Caffeine, a stimulant found in coffee and tea (which are often served to help a drowsy driver stay alert), cannot make a drunk driver sober. Studies show that caffeine does not improve an inebriated subject's driving (the result is a wide-awake drunk). Thus, a drunk driver, presumed to be sober after drinking a couple of cups of coffee, may get back on the road and become yet another highway statistic.

Marijuana is another mind-altering drug which can affect a wide range of skills needed for safe driving and quick thinking. Under the influence of this drug a person's reflexes are slowed, making it difficult for a driver to respond quickly to sudden and unexpected events. Marijuana can also affect a driver's ability to "track" (stay within the lane) through curves, to brake quickly, and to maintain appropriate speed and the proper distance between cars. Research clearly indicates that a normal level of driving performance is not regained for at least four to six hours after smoking a single marijuana cigarette. Drinking alcohol in combination with smoking marijuana greatly increases the risk of accidents.

Tranquilizers are central nervous system depressants (drugs which slow down the body). They are prescribed to help relieve tension and anxiety, but both major tranquilizers such as chlorpromazine (Thorazine) and minor ones such as diazepam (Valium) can have pronounced effects on driving skills. Studies show that prescribed doses of tranquilizers can affect driving skills by slowing reaction time and interfering with hand-eye coordination and judgment. Warnings that caution against taking medications while driving are often ignored.[7]

Recent research suggests that driving skills are most impaired during the first hour after a tranquilizer is taken. However, other drugs such as Flurazepam (Dalmane), a widely prescribed sleeping pill, accumulate in the body, and the resulting buildup can impair driving skills even the morning after the drug is taken. Elderly people must be especially careful when driving the day after taking this drug, because it may remain in their bodies even longer than is usual for younger people.

Other sedative or hypnotic drugs, including barbiturates and quaaludes, are powerful sedatives that calm people or help them sleep. Sleepy drivers are already a hazard on the road but mixing these drugs with alcohol can double the effects of both. If a physician prescribes a tranquilizer or sedative the individual must discuss with the doctor how the drug will affect their ability to drive safely.

Amphetamines, cocaine, and drugs often found in cold tablets and cough syrups such as phenylpropanolamine, ephedrine, and caffeine stimulate the central nervous system. While small amounts of these drugs generally make people who are tired feel more alert, repeated use of stimulants to combat fatigue will result in a loss of coordination. Heavy amphetamine use may keep an individual awake and active for long stretches of time but this individual may be edgy, less coordinated, and thus more likely to be involved in a traffic accident.

Nonprescription drugs such as cold tablets, cough syrups, allergy remedies, etc., that are purchased over the counter may contain antihistamines, alcohol, codeine, and other compounds that can be especially dangerous for drivers. Therefore, it is important that each person understand their reactions to the drugs they are using.

# Chapter 2

---

# The Effect of Alcohol on the Organs of the Body

Alcohol is a pleasant, relaxing, social beverage but it can also dull the brain and confuse physical reactions. It is a nutrient that provides more calories per ounce than any other food except fat, but it can actually increase the body's need for several essential vitamins and minerals. Current information about the benefits of alcohol is conflicting. There is evidence that for some people alcohol in very moderate amounts may increase their chances for a longer life. On the other hand, for those who have trouble controlling their drinking, even the smallest amount can mean disaster.[8]

For many who like an occasional drink but often find themselves drinking to excess, the question still remains: "Just how much is safe, and under what conditions?" We have known for a long time that alcohol is the only substance that can be absorbed directly into the bloodstream through the wall of the stomach. This immediate absorption means a drink will have an almost immediate effect. The speed with which alcohol enters the bloodstream is dependent upon how much food is in the stomach, especially fatty foods. Food prevents the alcohol from being absorbed into the bloodstream until all the food has been assimilated or at least broken down. But even if a few minutes are gained, some alcohol will inevitably enter the bloodstream within minutes of drinking it (see Charts 1 and 2 on pages 25–27).

# It Takes a Lot of Drink
# To Make A Drunk!

The examples which follow show the approximate *average* standard servings of liquor, beer or wine that a 150-pound person would have to consume in a one-hour period to reach 0.10%, the percentage-weight of alcohol in the bloodstream ("blood-alcohol concentration" or "BAC") that is the threshold of driver intoxication in most states.

Equivalent standard servings for "one drink" are: 1¼ ounces of 80-proof liquor, 4 ounces of normal-strength table wine, and 12 ounces of normal-strength beer.

To determine the approximate average number of standard drinks needed in a one-hour period to reach 0.10%, draw a line from BODY WEIGHT to 0.10%. The line will intersect the average number of ounces needed to produce 0.10%. Follow the same procedure to determine the amount of liquor needed to reach other blood-alcohol concentrations, such as 0.05%, 0.15%, etc.

Charts show *rough averages only.* Many factors affect the rate of alcohol absorption into the bloodstream. Amount of food consumed, kind of food and drink consumed, and percentage of fatty tissue in the body, for examples, can vary blood-alcohol concentration values.

*The rate of elimination of alcohol from the bloodstream is approximately 0.015% per hour. Therefore, subtract 0.015% from blood-alcohol concentration indicated on above charts for each hour after the start of drinking.

# Chart 1

**ESTIMATED AMOUNT OF 80 PROOF LIQUOR NEEDED TO REACH APPROXIMATE GIVEN LEVELS OF ALCOHOL IN THE BLOOD**

*"EMPTY STOMACH"*

**DURING A ONE-HOUR PERIOD***
**WITH LITTLE OR NO FOOD INTAKE PRIOR TO DRINKING**

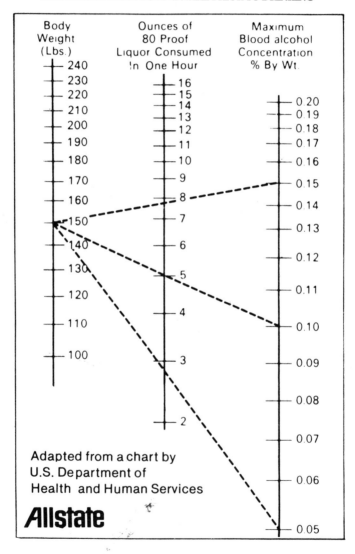

| Body Weight (Lbs.) | Ounces of 80 Proof Liquor Consumed In One Hour | Maximum Blood alcohol Concentration % By Wt. |
|---|---|---|

Adapted from a chart by
U.S. Department of
Health and Human Services

**Allstate**

# Chart 2

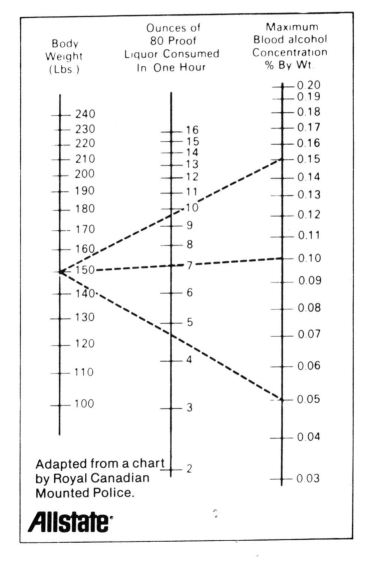

**"FULL STOMACH"**

**DURING A ONE-HOUR PERIOD\* OCCURRING BETWEEN ONE AND TWO HOURS AFTER AN AVERAGE MEAL**

Body
Weight
(Lbs.)

Ounces of
80 Proof
Liquor Consumed
In One Hour

Maximum
Blood alcohol
Concentration
% By Wt.

Adapted from a chart
by Royal Canadian
Mounted Police.

**Allstate®**

27

The liver, which normally processes fat and converts it into calories, also processes alcohol. Here, a series of steps occurs that breaks the alcohol down into water and carbon dioxide, providing seven calories per gram of alcohol during this metabolic process. After leaving the liver, alcohol is then disseminated to other vital organs including the lungs, brains, and kidneys. In the brain, alcohol anesthetizes the frontal lobe, which controls inhibitions, judgment, visual perception, and decision making.

But while the liver is breaking down alcohol, fat is building up. As drinking persists over a long period of time, fat accumulates in the liver. If drinking is discontinued, the fat buildup will subside, but if heavy drinking persists, the fat squeezes the liver cells, circulation ceases, and cirrohsis of the liver results. However, some experts agree that irreversible brain damage can occur before the advent of cirrohsis of the liver. In addition, heavy drinkers have an increased risk of cancer of the liver, mouth, and esophagus, especially if they are smokers as well. Alcohol consumption also promotes cancer of the lungs, pancreas, intestines, and prostate gland.

Alcohol consumption in the United States averages 2.8 gallons of pure alcohol a year for every drinker. That means that the ninety-five million Americans who drink are getting between ten and twenty percent of their calories from alcohol. But because they are not getting essential nutrients in the same proportion, their diet must be supplemented if they are to maintain good health. Moreover, these individuals must remember that their need for certain nutrients may actually increase because drinking depletes vitamin B, Niacin, Thiamin, Folacin, and B-12, as well as the minerals potassium, zinc, and magnesium.

However, a number of studies have shown that in very moderate amounts alcohol may be helpful, especially to the heart and cardiovascular system. Why moderate drinkers seem to have fewer heart attacks is unknown. It is known that alcohol raises the blood level of high-density lipoproteins, which are thought to help prevent the buildup of cholesterol in the arteries. Therefore, cholesterol related heart attacks might be less for those that imbibe moderately.

Just how much alcohol is safe varies with the person. If you smoke heavily, have a history of diseases associated with alcohol, overdrink, pregnant, or lactating, any alcohol may be too much for you. In any case, you should check with your physician to make sure that the risks do not outweigh the possible benefits.

# Chapter 3

## The Problem

Drunk driving continues to be one of our nation's most serious public health and safety problems. Some fifty percent of all drivers killed each year have a BAC in excess of the legal limit of 0.10 percent. In single-vehicle fatal crashes where fault can be pinpointed more accurately, upwards of sixty-five percent of those drivers who die were legally drunk. Over the past ten years the proportion of highway deaths involving alcohol has averaged a staggering 25,000 fatalities per year. This represents one-quarter of a million Americans who have lost their lives in alcohol-related crashes in the last decade. The associated costs of drunk driving accidents represents a high loss to our economy as well. A conservative estimate of the total costs of drunk driving in terms of insurance payments and medical fees is put at twenty-four billion dollars. According to the estimate of a major automobile insurer, one out of every four auto insurance premium dollars may go to pay for damage to people and property caused by drunk driving.

## Alcohol and Crashes

Alcohol is the major contributing factor in fatal automobile crashes. According to a 1978 review of the literature, approximately sixty percent of fatal crashes involved a driver who had been drinking. Between forty and fifty percent of these crashes involved a driver who had a BAC greater than .10 percent. With regard to alcohol and responsibility for fatal crashes, the drinking driver is even more significant. In one study, drivers judged to be at fault in fatal crashes were six times more likely to have had a BAC greater than .10 percent alcohol in their blood than drivers judged not at fault for their crashes.

The relationship between crash responsibility and unacceptable alcohol levels is shown even more clearly in single-vehicle crashes; of the drivers who perished in such accidents, between sixty and seventy-five percent of them had a BAC greater than .10 percent.

## The Driving Population

These statistics suggest that the majority of alcohol-related fatalities are caused by problem drinkers. Approximately fifteen percent of crashes which involve drinking drivers who do not have a BAC greater than .10 percent may be caused by so-called "social drinkers." The majority of drivers either abstain altogether or are light-to-moderate drinkers; however, liberal estimates suggest that approximately ten to fifteen percent of the nation's drivers could be classified as being "problem drinkers."

According to Robert F. Borkenstein, Professor of Police Administration at Indiana University, there are seven categories of "drinking drivers":[9]

1. Drinking drivers who, though they are skillful drivers, drink heavily and regularly. Consequently, whenever these so-called "functional alcoholics" drink, their BACs are generally in the high ranges, even when they drive.

2. Drinking drivers who are not compulsive drinkers but who are overly aggressive and as a result are not good drivers under most circumstances. Alcohol takes them from bad to worse.

3. Drinking drivers to whom neither drinking nor driving is usually a problem. They will occasionally drive when they have had too much to drink.

4. Drinking drivers who are unusually sensitive to the effects of alcohol.

5. Drinking drivers who are learners or beginners in both drinking and driving. Because their experience and skill in each area are limited, their driving behavior may be uncertain and unpredictable. This category includes some teenagers.

6. Drinking drivers who, because of age or illness, are losing

or have lost their driving skills. Alcohol accentuates this loss.

7. Drinking drivers who have no problem with drinking or driving. They conscientiously and consistently manage to stay below the threshold of alcohol impairment when they drink and then drive.

According to Dr. Borkenstein, drinking drivers in category one are involved in a disproportionate number of fatal crashes. Their consistently high BAC when drinking and driving suggests alcoholism to some degree.

## Arrested Drunk Drivers

The average proportion of licensed drivers arrested for drunk driving over a one-year period is estimated to be one percent. This translates to approximately 1.3 million of the 130 million licensed drivers in America.

On a nightly basis, nationwide, approximately 3500 drivers are arrested for drunk driving with BACs greater than .10 percent. In fact, the average BAC of these drinking drivers is approximately .20 percent, double the level which indicates presumed intoxication. Estimating an average period of alcohol consumption to be four to five hours means that fatally injured drinking drivers must have consumed about fifteen drinks prior to becoming involved in an accident. These estimates were taken from a number of roadside surveys conducted in conjunction with the Alcohol Safety Action Project and funded by the National Highway Traffic and Safety Administration (NHTSA).

It is important to note that fifteen drinks of any kind are equivalent to one another. It is a common fallacy to suppose that a can of beer contains less alcohol than a mixed drink containing a shot of hard liquor. In fact, one twelve-ounce can of beer is equal to four ounces of wine or 1¼ ounces (one shot) of hard liquor.

## Deterrents

Several avenues of prevention or penalty have evolved in an effort to deal effectively with the problem of drinking drivers. These include: raising the drinking age to twenty-one, revoking driver's licenses on either a provisional (the driver may drive to and from work, treatment program, etc.) or absolute (no legal driving allowed) basis, and rehabilitation programs. Each of these alternatives has its positive and negative aspects. However, according to H. Laurence Ross, author of *Deterring The Drinking Driver*:

> The greater the perceived likelihood of apprehension, prosecution, conviction, and punishment, the more severe the perceived eventual penalty, and the more swiftly it is perceived to be administered, the greater will be the deterrent effect of the threat.[10]

In nine states that lowered the drinking age, and then raised it again, there was an average reduction of twenty-eight percent in nighttime fatal crashes among eighteen-to-twenty-one-year-old drivers. Setting the national drinking age at twenty-one is not intended to place the responsibility for the drunk driving problem solely on young people; it merely recognizes the need for a uniform approach to protecting a segment of our society which is overly involved in alcohol-related crashes, and to protect other motorists from this high-risk group.

The National Highway Traffic and Safety Administration (NHTSA) recommends that the drinking age be uniform in order to eliminate "blood borders." For example, the drinking age is twenty-one in Pennsylvania and New Jersey, but nineteen in New York. The New York Division of Alcoholism and Alcohol Abuse reports that thirty-nine percent of New Jersey drivers and forty-nine percent of Pennsylvania drivers involved in alcohol-related accidents were involved in these accidents in New York.

Studies conducted by the California Department of Motor Vehicles reveal a significant reduction in violations and crashes for those whose licenses are suspended or revoked for four years. They also show lower violation and crash rates for the revoked/suspended group than for similar persons referred to education or rehabilitation programs in lieu of loss of license.[11, 12]

One of the most frequently used approaches in dealing with drunk drivers is referral to education or rehabilitation programs. Such programs can provide early identification of problem drinkers, but offer little deterrence against the possibility of continued violations. Therefore, the impact of such programs is, at best, limited to changing the behavior of only some drunk drivers.

Studies by Ellingstad, Springer, Holden, Stewart, Struckman, and Johnson concluded:

1. Some educational programs have demonstrated effectiveness in terms of reducing drunk driving arrests for social drinkers.

2. Very few educational or therapy programs have had a significant impact on problem drinkers who drive in terms of reducing alcohol-related arrests. None of these programs can claim to have reduced alcohol-related crashes.

3. Only Disulfiram (Anatabuse) programs (i.e., programs

using this drug, which induces nausea, vomiting, and other adverse reactions when alcohol is consumed) have demonstrated any impact in terms of reducing drinking behavior among apprehended drinking drivers.[13]

From these findings, it must be concluded that, when used alone, these programs have little potential for solving the entire drunk-driving problem.

## Recommendations

The following recommendations were compiled from information contributed by U.S. insurance companies and non-profit, public-concern groups such as MADD and RID.

1. The minimum drinking age for all states should be standardized to twenty-one years of age.

2. Existing drunk driving laws should be strengthened from "presumptive" to "illegal per se" statutes. "Illegal" means it is an offense to drive or otherwise be in control of an automobile with a 0.10 percent or greater BAC.

3. A governmental source of compensation should be made available to cover financial losses of injured victims, and families of victims, of alcohol-related crashes.

4. Arresting officers should be empowered to confiscate a drunk driver's license if the BAC test is failed. If the arrestee refuses the test, the license should be sent to the Driver's License Agency (DLA), and a temporary issued in its place.

5. "Occupation-only" driver permits should be issued on a limited basis, at the discretion of the DLA.

6. All alcohol-related driving problems should be reported to the DLA.

7. Make it illegal to remove any information concerning alcohol from a DLA driving record for at least seven years.

8. Connect all DLAs with the National Driver Register (NDR). This would inhibit those with revoked licenses in one state to apply to another.

9. Provide a force of driver's license enforcement personnel assigned by the DLA to enforce driver's license revocation and restricted occupational license compliance.

10. Provide in the law for immediate seizure and impoundment for confiscation and public sale of any vehicles being driven illegally by a person whose license has been revoked or restricted for drunk driving, alcohol-related convictions, or refusal of a BAC test.

11. Require the DLA and the driver's automobile insurance company to exchange information concerning any history of DUI or other driver's license sanctions.[14]

12. Sanction removal of license plates from drivers who habitually drive after their license has been revoked in order to prevent them from using the vehicle.

13. Unalterable driver's licenses should be used which clearly indicate whether the driver is of drinking age by using a color code.

14. Alcohol-related crash victims should be allowed to file lawsuits against drinking establishments that serve alcoholic beverages to the intoxicated driver. (Dram Shop Legislation.)[15]

# Chapter 4

# Road Tests
# and Alcohol

We know that alcohol interferes with reflex action, slows reaction time, impairs judgment and muscular coordination, diminishes side vision, and hinders the ability to distinguish differences in light and sound. Further, because of its depressing effect on the brain, alcohol often makes the driver believe he is doing a better job than normal. Hence, the drunk driver is likely to take more chances on the road and to insist on driving instead of turning over the wheel to someone sober.

## Road Tests

Road tests show that alcohol does impair driving performance, but they do not explain how alcohol produces certain mental effects. In laboratory tests, however, the impairment of various driving skills while DUI has been precisely measured. The 1974 report, "Alcohol, Drugs, and Driving," prepared for the U.S. Department of Transportation, stated that alcohol affects the intricate division of attention between visual search-and-recognition tasks and tracking tasks required of drivers. This conclusion is supported by evidence that alcohol impairs the rate of information-processing, an important aspect of the necessary time-sharing of the driver's attention between several inputs. The phrase "visual-search-and-recognition task" simply means that driving requires continual observation of other vehicles, potential obstacles, stop lights and signs, and road conditions. Looking through the windshield is not enough; the driver must also rely on a rearview mirror and an occasional turn of the head to check the blind spot when changing lanes. All these visual procedures constitute a search-and-recognition task. The term "tracking task" simply means "using the steering wheel." What the eye sees through the windshield must be translated by the brain into corrective movements to the wheel to keep the vehicle in the proper lane of traffic and to accurately negotiate curves and turns.

"Time sharing" can be translated as doing several things at once. Driving is a time-sharing activity, requiring the brain to divide its attention between search and recognition and tracking. Different bits of incoming information must be analyzed in a computer-like fashion, then various decisions must be made and executed.[16]

## What the Tests Show

A person visiting an optometrist for an eye examination is asked to read letters from a chart on the wall. The ability to see the letters clearly is referred to as "static visual acuity" and the ability to clearly see objects in motion is called "dynamic visual acuity." Static visual acuity is not greatly affected by alcohol in that the eye's ability to resolve images clearly is not impaired *if the visual target is standing still*. But dynamic visual acuity is very important for driving, and is impaired at blood levels as low as 0.02 percent in some subjects. In other words, at one-fifth the blood-alcohol level need for a drunk driving conviction, after as little as one drink, a driver's ability to see and distinguish moving objects will be impaired.

"Dark adaptation" refers to the ability to see clearly at low light levels such as exist when driving at night. The ability to detect low contrast, low illumination targets is usually impaired at blood alcohol levels of 0.08 percent or higher.

"Peripheral vision" refers to what is commonly known as seeing out of the corner of the eye. Researchers have found that peripheral vision is impaired by ten percent at blood-alcohol levels of 0.05 percent and by twenty-eight percent at levels of 0.10 percent. They have concluded that the effect of alcohol on peripheral vision is a function of the information load on central vision. From the standpoint of search and recognition, this means the impaired driver is faced with a much greater likelihood of an accident than if he were stone sober; however, tracking and time sharing will also affect the outcome of this situation.

As an example, if a driver is approaching a dimly lit intersection controlled by a traffic light at night, and the driver has had two beers (BAC is about 0.05 percent), the following might happen: as the driver approaches the intersection the signal is green but another car enters the intersection from the other street, running the red light. Will an accident occur? The driver at the green light has been drinking and his ability to see the approaching car is impaired because he is concentrating on steering his own car. The ability of his eyes to follow the other car is impaired, as is the ability to see it clearly. The question of whether an accident will occur depends on many other factors. How quickly will the driver react after seeing the other car? How quickly can his foot reach the brake pedal?

The key ingredient in this situation is "reaction time," defined as the time taken to initiate a response. In the laboratory, reaction time appears not to be greatly affected by small and moderate doses of alcohol so that in a simple reaction-time experiment the subject will not take any longer to press a button when a light flashes. However, individual functions tested separately often do not show much alcohol impairment, while functions combined into a complex task are highly susceptible to alcohol's effect.

Road tests designed to measure reaction time have yielded contradictory information. One test reported no increase in the time taken to initiate a lane-change maneuver when a light flashed. However, drivers with alcohol in their bloodstream made more tracking errors when executing the maneuver. Another test found a thirty-five percent increase in braking resistance when drivers reached blood alcohol levels of 0.01 percent. Yet according to the American Council on Alcohol, the question of alcohol impairing reaction time has not been answered conclusively. It seems reasonable to conclude that since defensive reaction to a crisis situation depends upon time sharing between visual and motor functions, reaction time must be impaired by alcohol in practical application (information obtained from the American Council of Alcohol Problems).

## Summation

As was stated earlier, alcohol is a mind-altering drug with an effect similar to sleeping pills and tranquilizers, which acts as a central nervous system depressant. In large quantities, alcohol can induce stupor and sleep, though in social settings, small doses tend to produce a kind of stimulation. This apparent stimulation results from the loss of inhibitions, caused by the depressant action of alcohol. This effect, in addition to producing sedation and increased fatigue, will also produce inattention and drowsiness which, of course, lead to a greater likelihood of insufficient response in a driving emergency. According to the National Council on Alcohol (NCA), the disinhibitory effect of alcohol will often result in fear reduction and increased assertiveness. Thus, a driver may take more risks. One of the most common effects of drinking is the mistaken belief that a person's driving ability remains unimpaired. Drivers on the test course reported the feeling of driving as well as if sober, even when pylons were knocked over and other performance results proved contradictory! It appears that alcohol impairs the emotional, psychological, and physiological requisites for safe driving.

# Chapter 5

# Emotions
# and Your Driving

An article written by R. H. Felix, M.D. when he was the director of the National Institute of Mental Health relates how a youthful driver was so infuriated at the failure of an oncoming motorist to dim his bright lights that he crashed head-on into the car, killing everyone in both cars except himself. The driver claimed he was trying to teach the driver of the oncoming car a lesson. This, of course, is an extreme example of the effect emotions can have on behavior. Research points out that traffic accidents and a good deal of unsafe driving can be attributed to many emotional factors.[17] Consider, for example, the following short article from the *Marin Independent Journal:*

### Alcoholics Profiled as Car Crash Cause

Psychiatrists have developed a profile of the alcoholic drinker at highest risk of causing auto accidents, and they say their findings should help in the campaign against drunken driving.

According to the investigators, the alcoholics most likely to be involved in personal-injury motor vehicle accidents share a history of early drinking, frequent job loss, and childhood fighting. These traits increase by more than seven times the risk that an alcoholic will cause an injurious traffic accident if the person is driving while drunk.

Dr. William Yates reported at the annual meeting of the American Psychiatric Association that "a high-risk group of alcoholic drivers may exist for focused attention in tackling the drunk driving problem." More than half the alcoholics he studied who had all three characteristics have been involved in personal-injury accidents while drunk, compared to only seven percent of those alcoholics who had none of the traits.

Yates and psychiatrists Russell Noyes of Iowa and Fred Petty of Texas studied 262 alcoholics admitted to the Veterans Administration Medical Center in Knoxville, Iowa for an intensive six-week alcoholism program. Of those, fifty-seven had been in personal-injury traffic accidents while driving when intoxicated. Comparing the fifty-seven with the 205 alcoholics with no history of accidents, Yates found that those involved in accidents:

1. Had started drinking at age sixteen, more than three years earlier than alcoholics who had no history of accidents. They also had begun drinking heavily much earlier in life, before age twenty as compared to over age twenty-six.

2. Were twice as likely to have experienced frequent job changes and unemployment, and more than twice as likely to have lost a job because of drinking.

3. Were ten times more likely to have been involved in frequent fighting in childhood.

4. Those in the accident group "lost control" of their drinking at a younger age, drank daily more frequently and used other drugs like marijuana more often.

5. These alcoholics, too, were more often diagnosed by doctors as suffering from anti-social personality, which is defined as an incapacity to understand or practice social values.

"Violent behavior as a child and while intoxicated appear to be risk factors for violent behavior on the road when intoxicated," says Yates. "Alcoholics who are able to maintain steady jobs and marriages appear to have a lower risk of accident behavior."[18]

According to the Eno Foundation for Highway Traffic Control, more attention needs to be given to the attitude of drivers. The foundation suggests that a significant percentage of accident repeaters appear maladjusted or emotionally disturbed. The disturbances mentioned are referred to as short-term or acute occurrences. Some examples of these reflect the everyday concerns we all have, but some can be emotionally debilitating: finances, death in the family, illness, marital problems, job-related stress, etc. In addition, there are other potential hazards such as the person who has had an argument at home or at the office, and jumps into the car and drives off in anger, or the teenager who has reluctantly been allowed to use the family car, after a long "hassle," and drives off full of frustration and resentment.

Such situations are recognizable to most of us. We know outwardly what we are angry about and hopefully our anger will fade before damage occurs. In a school for first offenders evidence demonstrated (conclusively) that these types of situations preceded the consumption of alcohol, and this drinking produced a BAC at the time of arrest in excess of .10 percent. Over fifty percent of the students stated they had an emotional upset prior to drinking and driving.

Another group of emotionally disturbed drivers are those who are unable to recognize their emotions and are deemed "chronic." They are widespread. We are all familiar with the driver who cannot stand to wait in long lines or be held up by a red light. He runs red lights, passes on the right when he should not, jumps the gun on the green light, and may even pass on a hill. Then there is the driver who feels other drivers are "taking advantage" of him, so he cuts in and tries to take advantage of the other person first. Or he may cut in simply to show off a new or more powerful car. Such drivers throw caution to the wind and any one who gets in their way will certainly be in danger.

Driver temperament is a factor in both safe and poor driving habits. The tense person who drives himself hard is not comfortable unless he is ahead. If he is thwarted in his efforts to move at his preferred pace, he becomes bored and angry and sits on the horn. This behavior is also characteristic of people who are on a rigid schedule and allow inadequate time for travel. When delayed, they become angry and frustrated and put unreasonable demands on themselves and others.

Other types include the controller, the absent-minded driver, the indecisive driver, and the thoughtless driver. The controller is all for enforcing rules and regulations that do not concern him. He might ride your tail because he believes slow drivers cause more accidents, or he might drive slowly because he feels everyone ought to drive more slowly. The absent-minded driver is preoccupied. The indecisive driver lacks experience and makes other drivers nervous because they do not know what he is going to do next. The thoughtless driver will not help someone out in a tight spot.

These are but a few examples of how emotions can affect our driving habits. According to Dr. Felix, we must be aware of our emotional makeup and take appropriate steps to guard against dangerous situations. If you know your limitations you can make appropriate allowances. Handicapped persons know their limitations; likewise, the able-bodied person must also know his limitations and handicaps when behind the wheel of a car. After all, consider the role of emotions as outlined in the following prediction which recently appeared in the *San Francisco Examiner*:

## U.S. Fans Could Turn Violent Too

In the week of May 25th, 1985, the worst soccer violence ever seen occurred in the European championships in Brussels, Belgium, in which thirty-eight spectators were killed. According to Denis Waitley, a leading sports psychologist, this event could very well happen in the United States within the next five to ten years.

Dr. Bruce Ogilvie, a San Jose State professor, stated that such a tragedy would be most likely to occur in Eastern and Southern cities. Sports psychologist Robert Case of Tulane University, and Tara Scanlan, past president of the North American Society for the Psychology of Sports and Physical Activity, believe that increasing violence among athletes prompts similar behavior among fans. Ogilvie believes that deep resentment stemming from working-class fans' socioeconomic miseries lies behind their violence. He said the primary cause of the Belgium tragedy which killed thirty-eight and injured 454 others was a "release of aggression reflecting alcohol use. You have a high proportion of people between the ages of eighteen and twenty-eight who feel an underlying rage about social and economic circumstances, booze, and this neurotic identification with a team."

Ogilvie further states, "People lose their identity in a movement, a faith, a team, almost anything." "They become children," said San Jose University sports psychologist Thomas Tutko. "The individuals who do this ordinarily have weak egos. They are childlike. They start drinking and it lowers their inhibitions."[19]

# Chapter 6

# Driving
# Under the Influence

Legislation enacted at the federal level in 1984 requires that
states either raise their minimum legal drinking age to twenty-
one or face the withholding of highway construction funds.
The new law, PL98-363, requires that states which do not have

a twenty-one-year-old drinking age law now in effect should pass such a law by September 30, 1986; states that do not comply will have five percent of highway construction funds withheld in 1987, and an additional ten percent withheld in 1988. Those states that pass drinking age laws in 1988 will have their 1987 funds released.

In addition to the minimum drinking age provisions, the new law contains a number of other highway safety provisions. It allots money for computerizing traffic records and developing comprehensive state child-passenger safety programs. It also allots funds for research into treatment/rehabilitation programs for convicted drunk drivers or the establishment of research programs for the detection of drunk drivers.

Further, the new law provides for a separate five percent grant to states that enact all of the following drunk driving penalties: minimum ninety-day license revocation and either 100 hours of community service or a forty-eight hour jail sentence for first offenders within five years of a first conviction; three-year license revocation and 120 days in jail for repeat offenders, and extended license revocation and thirty days in jail for driving with a revoked license.[20]

The campaign to encourage enactment of these laws is spearheaded by Mothers Against Drunk Drivers (MADD), the National Safety Council, Remove Intoxicated Drivers (RID), The National Parent-Teacher's Association (PTA), The National Council on Alcoholism, and Secretary of Transportation Elizabeth H. Dole. MADD founder Candy Lightner reported that there are 106 "Blood Borders," representing fifty-six percent of the total borders in this country that separate states with different drinking age laws.

Response from states to the passage of PL98-363 has been mixed. In all states the dollar amount at stake is a significant portion of their overall highway construction effort. Thus, it is expected that most states will choose to comply with the law, although some will do it grudgingly. Nebraska, Rhode Island, and Tennessee all raised their drinking age to twenty-one. Currently, twenty-three states have passed twenty-one-year-old drinking age laws; ten of those have been passed since 1982.

The fact is that in one-third of all fatal accidents involving sixteen-to-twenty-year-olds, the drivers had been drinking. While sixteen-to-twenty-four-year-olds are only twenty percent of the licensed driver population, those in this age group who drink account for forty-two percent of alcohol-related fatal crashes in the United States. This figure is two times higher than the alcohol-related accident rate among twenty-five to forty-four-year-olds. These statistics certainly seem to support legislation that will prevent an already accident-prone age group from drinking (see Charts 3 and 4, pages 54 and 55).

Chart 3

# Fatal Accident Involvement
# Rates by Driver

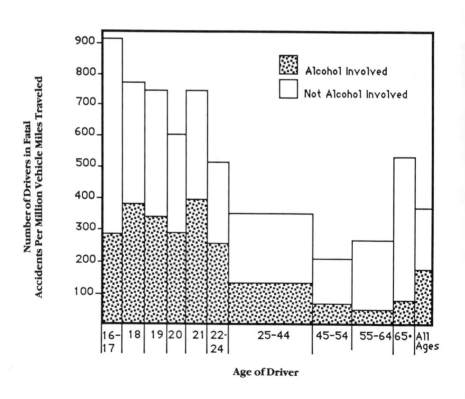

**Chart 4**

# Alcohol in Fatal Accidents for Various Age Groups

| Driver Age | % of Licensed Drivers[1] | 100 Million Vehicle Miles Travelled (VMT)[2] | | % of Drivers with Alcohol in Fatal Accidents (15 States) | National Estimates of Drinking Drivers In Fatal Accidents | | Number of Drivers in Fatal Accidents Per 100 Million (VMT)[3] | |
|---|---|---|---|---|---|---|---|---|
| | | Number | Percent | | Number | Percent | Alcohol | No Alcohol |
| 16-17 | 2.8 | 295 | 2.0 | 32 | 850 | 4.1 | 2.9 | 6.2 |
| 18-20 | 6.9 | 1061 | 7.0 | 47 | 3350 | 15.9 | 3.2 | 3.6 |
| 21 | 2.6 | 349 | 2.3 | 53 | 1320 | 6.3 | 3.8 | 3.4 |
| 22-24 | 7.9 | 1266 | 8.4 | 51 | 3330 | 15.8 | 2.6 | 2.5 |
| 25-44 | 42.9 | 7081 | 46.9 | 41 | 9340 | 44.3 | 1.3 | 1.9 |
| 45-54 | 13.3 | 2648 | 17.6 | 32 | 1590 | 7.5 | 0.6 | 1.3 |
| 55-64 | 12.4 | 1619 | 10.7 | 21 | 830 | 3.9 | 0.5 | 1.9 |
| 65+ | 11.2 | 770 | 5.1 | 12 | 470 | 2.2 | 0.6 | 4.5 |
| **TOTAL** | **100.0%** | **15,089** | **100.0%** | **40** | **21,000** | **100.0%** | **1.4** | **2.2** |

1 Highway Statistics 1982, Federal Highway Administration, Washington, D.C. 1983
2 1977 National Personal Transportation Survey, FHWA, Washington, D.C., 1980
3 The number of drivers in fatal accidents per 100 million vehicle miles traveled is found by dividing the number of drivers in fatal accidents who are in that age group by the VMT for that age group (in hundreds of millions).

## California Drunk Driving Laws

The drunk-driving laws currently in effect in the State of California are a good example of legislation that meets the problem of drunk driving head-on. This state's DUI laws are tough, and the more they are broken, the tougher they become on the individual. The new laws, which have been in effect since January 1, 1982, increase the probability that anyone charged with driving under the influence of alcoholic beverages will be convicted. They also assure that DUI offenders will pay stiffer fines, be subject to vehicle impoundment, have their driver's licenses suspended or revoked, and spend more time in jail. The most significant aspects of these laws makes it a crime for a motor vehicle operator to drive when his/her BAC is 0.10 percent or higher. In other words, if you have enough drinks to raise your BAC to 0.10 percent or higher, and you get in a vehicle and drive, you are violating the law.

According to the California Highway Patrol, every DUI conviction will result in a mandatory minimum jail sentence ranging from forty-eight hours in a county jail to four years in a state penitentiary. The one exception to this is the case of a misdemeanor first offense where a judge may, at his discretion, substitute for a jail term required attendance at a drunk driver school and a ninety-day license suspension (the offender is given permission to drive only to and from work and a treatment program). Every DUI conviction will have a mandatory minimum fine of $390, except for a third felony which causes bodily injury and occurs within five years of two previous DUI offenses. When probation is denied on such a conviction, the mandatory minimum fine is $1,015.

In the case of a second, or subsequent, conviction, a judge may require verified attendance for one full year at an alcohol treatment program, adding jail time as a deterrence against nonattendance.

If a vehicle involved in any DUI violation is registered to the convicted driver, it may be impounded at the driver's expense for a period of one to ninety days.

If for any reason a judge dismisses or reduces a DUI to a lesser charge, he must read his reason for doing so into the court records, which will remain a part of the driver's permanent record. In a misdemeanor DUI case, plea bargaining may be possible; yet even if a DUI charge is reduced to reckless driving, the prosecutor may note on the record that alcohol was involved in the case. In any subsequent charges against the same defendant, reckless driving with alcohol involvement will count the same as a prior DUI conviction.

If a driver with two prior DUI convictions is found guilty on a DUI felony charge and denied probation, he or she will serve a mandatory two-to-four-year term in a state penitentiary, pay a minimum fine of $1,015, and have driving privileges revoked for five years (see Chart 5, page 58).

Chart 5

# DUI Laws of California

| | FIRST CONVICTION | SECOND CONVICTION (within 5 years) | THIRD CONVICTION (within 5 years) | FOURTH OR MORE CONVICTION (within 5 years) |
|---|---|---|---|---|
| **DRIVING UNDER THE INFLUENCE (MISDEMEANOR)** | Probation Granted (3 years)<br><br>Fine $390 – $1,000<br>Driver Improvement and/or Alcohol Treatment Program<br>County jail 48 hours – 6 months or 90-day license restriction (to and from work and treatment program and within scope of employment)<br><br>No Probation<br><br>Fine $390 – $1,000<br>County jail 96 hours – 6 months<br>6 month license suspension on court order | Probation Granted (3 years)<br><br>Fine $390 – $1,000<br>County jail 48 hours – 1 year<br>Alcohol Treatment Program (1 year)<br>1 year license restriction<br>or<br>Fine $390 – $1,000<br>County jail 10 days – 1 year<br>1 year license suspension<br>Alcohol Treatment Program (1 year)<br><br>No Probation<br><br>Fine $390 – $1,000<br>County jail 90 days – 1 year<br>1 year license suspension | Probation Granted (3 years)<br><br>Fine $390 – $1,000<br>County jail 120 days – 1 year<br>1 year Alcohol Treatment Program (if no previous participation)<br>3 years license revocation<br><br>No Probation<br><br>Fine $390 – $1,000<br>County jail 120 days – 1 year<br>3 years license revocation | Probation Granted (3 years)<br><br>Fine $390 – $1,000<br>County jail 180 days – 1 year<br>1 year Alcohol Treatment Program (if no previous participation)<br>4 year license revocation<br><br>No Probation<br><br>Fine $390 – $1,000<br>County jail 180 days – 1 year<br>4 year license revocation |

| | FIRST CONVICTION | SECOND CONVICTION (within 5 years) | THIRD OR MORE CONVICTION (within 5 years) | |
|---|---|---|---|---|
| **DRIVING UNDER THE INFLUENCE, RESULTING IN INJURY (FELONY)** | Probation Granted (3 years)<br><br>Fine $390 – $1,000<br>County jail 5 days – 1 year<br>1 year license suspension<br>Alcohol or Drug Education Program<br><br>No Probation<br><br>Fine $390 – $1,000<br>State prison or county jail<br>90 days – 1 year<br>1 year license suspension | Probation Granted (3 years)<br><br>Fine $390 – $1,000<br>County jail 30 days – 1 year<br>1 year Alcohol Treatment Program (if no previous participation)<br>1 year license suspension plus 2 years restriction<br>or<br>Fine $390 – $5,000<br>County jail 120 days minimum<br>3 years license revocation<br><br>No Probation<br><br>Fine $390 – $5,000<br>State prison or county jail<br>120 days – 1 year<br>3 years license revocation | Probation Granted (3 years)<br><br>Fine $390 – $5,000<br>County jail 1 year minimum<br>1 year Alcohol Treatment Program (if no previous participation)<br>Make restitution to victim(s) or victim's family or reparation for damages<br>5 years license revocation<br><br>No Probation<br><br>Fine $1,015 – $5,000<br>State prison 2, 3, 4 years<br>5 years license revocation | |

The California Department of Motor Vehicles distributes charts that calculate a person's BAC relative to time and weight (see Charts 6 and 7, pages 60–62).[21]

# Chart 6

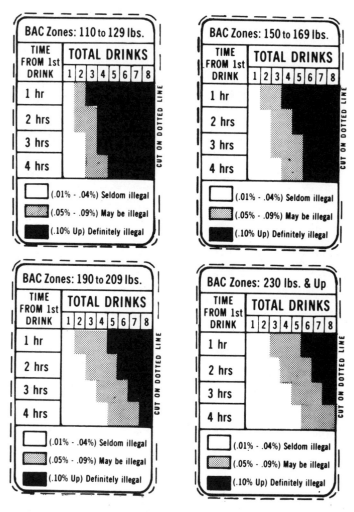

*There is no safe way to drive after drinking.* These charts show that a few drinks can make you an unsafe driver. They show that drinking affects your **BLOOD ALCOHOL CONCENTRATION (BAC).** The **BAC** zones for various numbers of drinks and time periods are printed in white, grey, and black. **HOW TO USE THESE CHARTS:** First, find the chart that includes your weight. For example, if you weigh 160 lbs., use the "150 to 169" chart. Then look under "Total Drinks" at the "2" on this "150 to 169" chart. Now look below the "2" drinks, in the row for 1 hour. You'll see your **BAC** is in the grey

# Chart 7

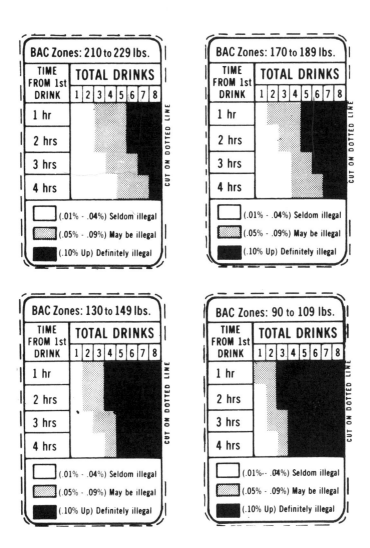

| BAC Zones: 210 to 229 lbs. | | | | | | | | |
|---|---|---|---|---|---|---|---|---|
| TIME FROM 1st DRINK | TOTAL DRINKS | | | | | | | |
| | 1 | 2 | 3 | 4 | 5 | 6 | 7 | 8 |
| 1 hr | | | | | | | | |
| 2 hrs | | | | | | | | |
| 3 hrs | | | | | | | | |
| 4 hrs | | | | | | | | |

☐ (.01% - .04%) Seldom illegal
▨ (.05% - .09%) May be illegal
■ (.10% Up) Definitely illegal

| BAC Zones: 170 to 189 lbs. | | | | | | | | |
|---|---|---|---|---|---|---|---|---|
| TIME FROM 1st DRINK | TOTAL DRINKS | | | | | | | |
| | 1 | 2 | 3 | 4 | 5 | 6 | 7 | 8 |
| 1 hr | | | | | | | | |
| 2 hrs | | | | | | | | |
| 3 hrs | | | | | | | | |
| 4 hrs | | | | | | | | |

☐ (.01% - .04%) Seldom illegal
▨ (.05% - .09%) May be illegal
■ (.10% Up) Definitely illegal

| BAC Zones: 130 to 149 lbs. | | | | | | | | |
|---|---|---|---|---|---|---|---|---|
| TIME FROM 1st DRINK | TOTAL DRINKS | | | | | | | |
| | 1 | 2 | 3 | 4 | 5 | 6 | 7 | 8 |
| 1 hr | | | | | | | | |
| 2 hrs | | | | | | | | |
| 3 hrs | | | | | | | | |
| 4 hrs | | | | | | | | |

☐ (.01% - .04%) Seldom illegal
▨ (.05% - .09%) May be illegal
■ (.10% Up) Definitely illegal

| BAC Zones: 90 to 109 lbs. | | | | | | | | |
|---|---|---|---|---|---|---|---|---|
| TIME FROM 1st DRINK | TOTAL DRINKS | | | | | | | |
| | 1 | 2 | 3 | 4 | 5 | 6 | 7 | 8 |
| 1 hr | | | | | | | | |
| 2 hrs | | | | | | | | |
| 3 hrs | | | | | | | | |
| 4 hrs | | | | | | | | |

☐ (.01%-- .04%) Seldom illegal
▨ (.05% - .09%) May be illegal
■ (.10% Up) Definitely illegal

shaded zone. This means that if you drive after 2 drinks in 1 hour, you could be arrested. In the grey zone, your chances of having an accident are 5 times higher than if you had no drinks. But, if you had 4 drinks in 1 hour, your **BAC** would be in the black shaded area . . . and your chances of having an accident 25 times higher. What's more, it is **ILLEGAL** to drive at this **BAC** (.10% or greater). Before reaching the white **BAC** zone again, the chart shows you would need 4 hours . . . with no more drinks.

**REMEMBER:** "One drink" is a 12-ounce beer, or a 4-ounce glass of wine, **or** 1¼-ounce shot of 80-proof liquor (even if it's mixed with non-alcoholic drinks). If you have larger or stronger drinks, or drink on an empty stomach, or if you are tired, sick, upset, or have taken medicines or drugs, you can be **UNSAFE WITH FEWER DRINKS.**

Permission for reprint granted by California Department of Motor Vehicles.

# Chapter 7

# Young People and Alcohol

## Alcohol Use in Fatal Accidents for Various Age Groups

James C. Fell of the National Highway Traffic Safety Administration (NHTSA)[22] states that reported blood alcohol levels for virtually all drivers killed in fatal crashes demonstrate that drivers between sixteen and twenty-four years of age have the highest accident rates (per mile traveled and per licensed driver). This is true despite the fact that only one-third of the sixteen- and seventeen-year olds involved in fatal crashes were drinking. This proportion of alcohol use rises with age to about one-half of the twenty-one to twenty-four-year-old drivers. After the age of twenty-five the proportion of drinking drivers in fatal crashes steadily declines to approximately twelve percent for drivers over sixty-four.

## The Drinking Chronicle of a Teenager

*The following drinking chronicle of a teenager is presented to illuminate the circumstances that can give rise to alcohol abuse by adolescents and the problems that can grow out of it. This is the actual story of a recovering alcoholic youth from a middle-class family—the son of an alcoholic father. The first-person narrative is taken from a talk he gave recently to a junior high school PTA in a Washington, D.C., suburb. At last report, the father was still drinking and the youth was living with another family.*

"I'm Charles, 17, a high school student and an alcoholic. I started drinking at the age of 12. I was hanging around with an older group of kids and I drank to be 'cool.' Nothing much happened from my drinking until I was 14. By that time I looked older than I was, and I could buy beer or liquor without any trouble. The summer before I entered the eighth grade I started working in a gas station in a neighborhood where the people were very alcohol-oriented. My boss drank a lot and he always had beer around the station. He encouraged me to drink . . . I changed a great deal that summer and took a turn toward alcohol. I changed my attitude towards other people, got sloppy and careless, and started getting into fights.

"By the time I started school that fall, I was drinking so much that I needed something every morning for some get-up-and-go. I started pitching in with other boys in the eighth grade to buy a case of beer so we could drink during school. We would hide it in some bushes near the school and go up there during recess. By lunch we would be pretty well totaled. The group of us started growing in number. The playground supervisor began wondering why half of the eighth grade were wandering up the hill during recess. Finally, he took a look—and found the beer. He let us off easy, just told us not to do it any-

more. When we asked him what to do with the left-over beer, he said to put it in his car . . . It was a fun year. I got drunk every weekend . . . It seemed like everybody in the eighth grade graduating class was drunk. One boy fell down as he was about to get his diploma.

"I left home that summer, caddied for a country club and lived in the clubhouse. At night, friends and I would go bar hopping. One night in a Washington bar, I got up to talk to a pretty girl who had smiled at me. The next thing I knew, I was coming to in an alley. . . .

"I moved back with my father and entered junior high school. I started smoking pot, but it was making me lose the desire to do things. So I cut it out and started drinking booze again. . . . By the time I got to the tenth grade, I was keeping a 6-pack of beer in my locker at all times. . . . I went out for the football team and would have been a starter if I hadn't been drinking. . . .

"I turned into a super-derelict. I didn't care about school or anything, just drinking. I started getting the DTs. I stayed drunk all the way through the next summer. In the fall, I went out for football again. The coach kept me on the bench most of the time because he knew I was drunk. He put me in one game at the very end as a fullback. I couldn't get going and about 20 guys piled on me. . . .

"It took an accident to get me straightened out. I was driving along and started to hallucinate and crashed into the median strip of a highway at about 50 miles an hour. I was knocked unconscious for about 10 minutes. When I came to, I decided it was time to do something about my drinking. Since I already belonged to Alateen, I knew about Alcoholics Anonymous and that's where I went for help. Now I haven't had a drink for 6 and a half months and I'm staying sober one day at a time."

Permission for reprint granted by the U.S. Department of Health and Welfare.

More teenagers than ever are drinking in a self-destructive manner. Teenage alcohol consumption threatens both their lives and the lives and property of others. The problem is so acute that both public and private agencies have initiated new alcohol treatment services and established prevention programs geared to the adolescent. New organizations have been developed by students themselves, such as Students Against Driving Drunk (SADD).

Research is under way to clarify the extent to which drinking and driving have increased among young people in an effort to determine more precisely what prevention and treatment strategies will be most appropriate. According to Dr. Morris E. Chafetz, "The most promising approaches to prevention are those which focus on promoting responsible decision making and the development of a healthy self-concept in young people. People in the helping professions must encourage teenagers to determine their identities by providing them with a wider range of information. The future, however, will be ominous if our young people do not adopt more responsible attitudes toward alcohol than today's adult population."[23]

According to an article in *Alcohol Health and Research World,* 1975, various studies have indicated that experimentation with alcohol has become almost universal among high school students. Results of a national survey conducted in 1974 for the National Institute on Alcohol Abuse and Alcoholism (NIAA) revealed that ninety-three percent of boys and eighty-seven percent of girls in their senior year of high school had experimented with alcohol, and more than half of the nation's seventh graders had tried drinking at least once during the previous year. Beer is the beverage most preferred, which is not surprising because the beer manufacturers' advertising budget today runs into the billions annually.

It appears young people today are experimenting with alcohol at increasingly early ages, according to a survey conducted by the National Commission on Marijuana and Drug Abuse. This survey indicated that alcohol use ranged from 46.3 to 72.9 percent for teenagers. Although experts cannot discern a clear relationship between age and drug experimentation, they hypothesize that earlier social maturation leads to earlier experimentation in a variety of adult behaviors. Young people drink for a variety of reasons; the most pervasive being parental role modeling and peer influences. Because parents serve as role models for adult behaviors, their attitudes and practices have a major influence in determining their children's attitudes toward alcohol use during adolescence. However, one of the most potent forces causing teenage drinking is peer pressure.

Another group of role models for young people are entertainers and professional athletes. Musicians with their lyrics of love, rejection, rebellion, and drugs offer "hope" to our young society. Retired athletes receive enormous sums of money to promote alcohol. Obviously, the alcohol industry does not overlook potential users on the horizon; this might explain why they invest huge sums of money to promote their products and provide such handsome incomes to celebrities.

To justify alcohol commercials, one sports columnist suggests that if beer commercials were banned from television, the next movement would be to enact an amendment to ban alcohol altogether. A similar argument is posed by a California wine industry official who suggests that as alcohol does not kill — it is the automobile that kills — the car should be banned. Most adolescents start out with beer and stay with it through life. If the country cannot make sound moral decisions in the face of overwhelming evidence that drinking and driving kills thousands of innocent people yearly, what will it take to solve this problem?

The alcohol industry has a great deal of money to oppose legislation that would decrease the exposure of their products to young people. According to University of Alabama sociologist Gerald Globetti, "Sooner or later, all young people in our society are faced with the inevitable decision to drink or not to drink. Three-fourths of them will make the decision to use alcohol before they are legally entitled. One-third will use alcohol on a regular basis, while five to ten percent will experience serious complications as a result of drinking, and one in twelve will go on to become adult problem drinkers or alcoholics."[24]

## Problem Drinkers Among Adolescents

Experts cannot agree precisely on the term "problem drinker" as it pertains to the adolescent; however, alcohol-related arrests of those under age eighteen increased nationally 135 percent between 1960 and 1973 for such offenses as public drunkenness, liquor violations (purchase and misuse), and crimes against persons or property. Arrests for teenage DUI during the same period rose an alarming 400 percent. The uniform crime report demonstrates a high correlation between alcohol abuse and increased detention and arrests for adolescents.

Alcohol-related problems at school are also increasing. Community resources dealing with acute alcohol problems include adult-oriented alcoholism treatment programs and Alcoholics Anonymous (AA). The Second Special Report to the U.S. Congress on Alcohol and Health from the Secretary of Health, Education, and Welfare noted that problem drinking among adolescents is often part of a pattern of deviant behavior. It has been widely accepted that children of alcoholic parents are especially vulnerable to the possibility of becoming alcohol abusers.

## Prevention

NIAAA Director of Prevention Donald G. Phelps stated, "Many of the same decision-making mechanisms involved in deciding how to use alcohol will be involved in deciding how to drive a car, how to handle finances, whom to marry, and how to plan for the future. These types of decisions should be inculcated into the education process early on in school, and reinforced by the parents." [25]

Dr. Globetti advocated introduction of alcohol education as early as the first grade. He states that children at six or seven years of age have some very clear notions about alcohol and its effects. The school is the logical place to initiate alcohol education and prevention, because it reaches more young people than any other single institution. However, before school-based alcohol education programs can be effective, teachers and adults who serve as role models must also be educated in dealing with the issues surrounding alcohol use and abuse. The family is considered by many authorities to be the most effective agent influencing the drinking habits of young people. However, as a group they seem to be the most resistant to providing help in alcohol prevention. Dr. Don Calahan, in his book *Problem Drinkers,* states: "Any effective campaign for moderation in drinking should be directed to parents to point out the dangers of a home atmosphere which is permissive of heavy drinking, and the effects it can have on young people." [26]

Youth-oriented programs have been instituted throughout the nation in recent years; most of these have been targeted to elementary and junior high school students. The emphasis of these programs has been to define the influence peer pressure has on chilren. Emphasis is also being placed on teaching young people decision-making skills. Older students are used as role models for the younger participants, and those students who are "natural" leaders are selected to receive training in developing responsible attitudes and skills in decision making which they can teach their peers.

A peer center prevention program in New York City's Harlem and East Harlem sections was initiated by a private social welfare agency, in cooperation with the New York schools, and funded by the NIAAA. The program was administered by Boy's Harbor, an organization which has been working with youth since 1937. The director, Robert North, explained that fourteen- to eighteen-year-old boys and girls who are identified as leaders by their peer groups are chosen from the public schools and from street gangs. They receive two to four months of training in group dynamics, problem solving techniques, responsible drinking attitudes, and facts about alcohol. These teenagers then develop their own curriculum on alcohol to be presented to the peer group, either in school health classes or informally in their gangs. It is believed that if teenagers can learn to make responsible decisions about the choices they face in growing up this is bound to promote the responsible use of alcohol and other drugs in their lives.

**Treatment Programs**

A number of adult-oriented alcohol treatment programs have added a youth component in response to the increasing demand for treatment of adolescents and teenagers. Crisis centers around the country that were originally established to combat drug abuse are now reorienting themselves to deal with the alcohol problem. Alateen, the youth component of Al-anon, a fellowship for relatives and friends of alcoholics, has recently been established as well. It serves as a major treatment resource for young people who have an alcoholic parent. In Alcoholics Anonymous, the median age of members has been gradually falling due to the number of teenage participants (which has sharply risen during the recent past). Dr.

Basil Clyman, director of the Alcohol Detoxification Center at the University of California Medical Center, proposed recovery homes for young alcohol abusers with staff members who are qualified, among others things, in adolescent psychology.

At the Alcoholism Center Coordinating Education, Prevention, and Treatment (ACCEPT) at New York City's Cabrini Center, young people from ages twelve to eighteen are treated for alcoholic-related problems in a hospital setting on both an in- and out-patient basis. The majority of the patients in ACCEPT are young alcohol abusers who show early symptoms of alcoholism. The center also provides treatment for non-alcoholic children who have been psychologically harmed by alcoholic parents. The center includes a broad range of treatment approaches, primarily emphasizing family counseling.

There are many other treatment programs throughout the United States funded by the NIAAA. The focus of these counseling services is education rather than confrontation. In additionto individual and family counseling, at these centers young residents are required to participate in academic studies. It appears that more segments of society are becoming involved in helping young people cope with their alcoholic problem. Dr. Morris E. Chafetz (NIAAA Director) stated, "Youths can come to understand the importance of responsible drinking by those who make the personal, private decision to take alcohol. Young people, after all, do have a sense of social responsibility, despite what we have heard and read in recent years. They are seeking answers, searching for adult roles which they can comfortably adopt. Most drinking by youth is a move toward adult patterns of behavior, not rebellion against parents. Because young people seek adult roles, we must be especially conscious of our actions even more than our words. What we do, by and large, they will do." [27]

# QUIZ

1. *America's teens*

   ☐ Are consuming less alcohol now than they did two years ago.

   ☐ Are consuming more alcohol now than they did two years ago.

   ☐ Are consuming the same amount of alcohol now as two years ago.

2. *Which of the following statements are true?*

   ☐ Marijuana use by 1984 high school seniors increased over previous years.

   ☐ Use of cocaine by 1984 high school seniors decreased.

   ☐ Multiple drug usage (use of more than one) is increasing.

3. *In the early 1970's more than half of the states in the United States lowered their legal minimum drinking age — most often from 21 to 18. By 1980, most had decided to raise them again, even though not all to 21. Why?*

   ☐ Significant increases were shown in alcohol fatalities for drivers under 21.

   ☐ Studies showed that over 700 lives of persons under 21 could be saved per year if the drinking age was raised to 21 throughout the country.

   ☐ Too many drunk driving crashes were occurring near state borders.

4. *What percentage of college undergraduates are "heavy drinkers" (56 or more drinks per month)?*

   ☐ 10%

   ☐ 20%

   ☐ 50%

5. *16 to 24 year olds hold 20% of the nation's drivers licenses. They are involved in what percentage of the fatal alcohol related crashes?*

   ☐ 20%

   ☐ 40%

   ☐ 50%

6. *Research has shown that the strongest predictor about an individual's decision about drinking and driving is*

   ☐ Peer pressure.

   ☐ One or both parents drink and drive.

   ☐ What the individual professes about drinking and driving when sober.

7. *(True/False) Traffic Accidents are the leading cause of death for 15-24 year olds in the United States.*

8. *What percentage of traffic fatalities are alcohol related?*
   ☐ 20%
   ☐ 50%
   ☐ 90%

9. *Statistically, the person at highest risk for being killed in a drunk driving crash is*
   ☐ a 21 year old female.
   ☐ a 19 year old male.
   ☐ a 16 year old male.

10. *Excessive use of alcohol:*
   ☐ Improves sexual drive.
   ☐ Reduces sexual drive leading to impotence.
   ☐ Has no effect on sexual performance.

11. *Which of the following drinks is most intoxicating?*
   ☐ a glass of table wine.
   ☐ a 12 oz. beer.
   ☐ one oz. of 86 proof liquor.

12. *If you weigh 125 pounds how many drinks can you have before your driving would be impaired?*
   ☐ 1
   ☐ 2
   ☐ 3

13. *If you weigh 125 pounds, how many drinks can you have before you are legally intoxicated and may be charged with DWI if you drive?*
   ☐ 1
   ☐ 2
   ☐ 3

14. *(True/False) Usually, if a person under 21 kills someone while driving drunk, he will not be punished because he is still a minor.*

15. *Which of the following have been found to be effective means of decreasing drunk driving crashes?*
    ☐ Information about DWI laws and alcohol's effect on driving ability.
    ☐ Strict uniform enforcement of DWI laws which jail all offenders, including teens.
    ☐ Making plans *before* drinking for getting home.
    ☐ Teen curfews.

16. *Smoking a marijuana joint is*
    ☐ More hazardous than smoking a pack of cigarettes.
    ☐ Less hazardous than smoking a pack of cigarettes.
    ☐ About the same risk as smoking a pack of cigarettes.

# ANSWERS TO QUIZ

1. America's teens are consuming *more* alcohol now than they did two years ago. A Gallup Poll Survey published in September, 1984, reports that *6 out of 10* youths between 13 and 18 are drinkers. This is up *20%* from 1982 figures. Of the teen drinkers, 20% drink at least once a week and consume 5 to 12 drinks at a time. (Source: The Gallup Poll, September, 1984, and the National Federation of Parents for Drug Free Youth.)

2. Multiple drug usage is increasing. In the last three years multiple addiction has risen from 24% to 40%. Nearly half of teenage males who kill themselves or others in a highway crash have alcohol and marijuana or alcohol and cocaine in their blood. Marijuana usage by high school seniors, however, is down — only 5% say they use it daily. 10% reported daily use in 1978. Cocaine use has remained constant since 1978 — 6% use it monthly. (Source: Alcoholics Anonymous Survey, 1983; Michigan Institute for Social Research, 1984; Insurance Institute for Highway Safety, 1984.)

3. All are true. For a synopsis of this issue, see *U.S. News and World Report,* January, 1984.

4. According to a University of Cincinnati survey in 1983, 21% (correct answer 20%) admitted to having 56 or more drinks per month. Carol Sussman, a press officer at the National Institute on Drug Abuse says that one of every 16 *junior high* and *high school* students drink every day. College sophomores drink nearly twice as much as college freshmen, juniors or seniors. (Source: Student Press, Washington, D.C., Feb. 15, 1984; Temple University Survey, 1984.)

5. It has been well established that this age group is involved in 42% (correct answer is 40%) of fatal alcohol related crashes. (Source: Report of Presidential Commission on Drunk Driving, December, 1983.)

6. Peer pressure to drink and drive remain the strongest predictor, but parental influence runs a close second. Teenagers learn drinking and driving by first riding with a drinking driver. (See 1978 Research Triangle Institute Study of 10th to 12th graders. This study was funded by the National Institute on Drug Abuse. Also reference North, R., and Aronge, R., Jr. *Teenage Drinking: The Number One Threat to Young People Today.* New York: Collier Books, 1980; Hartford, T.C. "Ecological Factors in Drinking" in Blane, H.T., and Chaftex, M.E., eds., *Youth, Alcohol, and Social Policy,* New York: Pelnum Press, 1979; and Rachal, J.V., et al., *A National Study of Adolescent Drinking Behavior, Attitudes and Correlates.* (Rockville, MD; National Institute on Alcohol Abuse and Alcoholism, 1975); Nuskamer, M., and Zuzman, M., "Autos, Alcohol, and Adolescence: Forgotten Concerns and Overlooked Linkages," Journal of Drug Education 11(2), 1981.)

7. True. (Source: *Fourth Special Report to the U.S. Congress on Alcohol and Health from the Secretary of Health and Human Services,* Washington, D.C.; National Institute on Alcohol Abuse and Alcoholism, 1981.) Traffic accidents are the *overall* leading cause of death among 15 to 24 year olds. While all other causes of death for this age group continue to decrease, highway fatalities continue to increase. (Source: National Center for Health Statistics, 1980.)

8. 50% or 90% is correct. Many studies, for example the 1981 NIAAA study cited above, show a range of 40% to 55% of fatally injured drivers have blood alcohol contents of at least .10 percent. However, a recent study of the College of American Pathologists (medical examiners) has shown that 90% of traffic fatalities involve drunk drivers. (Skokie, Illinois: College of American Pathologists, Dec., 1983.)

9. 19 year old male. (Source: *Fatal Accident Reporting System,* National Highway Traffic Safety Administration census of fatal accidents in 1978 and 1980.)

10. 70% to 80% of male alcoholics show reduced sexual drive or impotence. (Source: *Alcohol and Health,* Report of the Secretary of Health and Human Services, December, 1982.)

11. All are the same.

12. 1

13. 3

14. False. Most states provide for 17 year olds and above to be certified as adults for criminal cases if the judge so determines. In Texas, a high school senior was recently sentenced to two years in prison after being convicted of involuntary manslaughter. He had been put on probation 16 days before the fatal crash for misdemeanor driving while intoxicated. He said he didn't think the probation was "anything that serious."

15. All are correct. Recent studies show that a *credible, deterrent threat* is effective. Teenagers say if they know that there is a good chance they will get caught drinking and driving *and* that there is a good chance they will be punished (not lectured or warned) they believe they would stop. Teen curfews in New York and Louisiana have lowered licensing rates and therefore crash rates. 90% of the students interviewed favored a curfew law.

16. Smoking a marijuana joint is about equal to smoking one pack of cigarettes a day. (Source: Dr. Alfred Munzer, Takoma Park, MD, lung specialist, *Pulsebeats,* January, 1985.)

# Chapter 8

# Helping Agencies

### The National Council on Alcoholism

The National Council on Alcoholism (NCA) is located in most metropolitan centers of the United States. It is a voluntary (nongovernmental), nonprofit health agency supported by a variety of sources, including private gifts, contributions, foundation grants, government grants, and government contracts. It is run by citizens who volunteer their time to conduct programs in education, advocacy, information, and referral, and to assist the development of community resources and services aimed at prevention and reduction of alcoholism. The council's goals are wide and varied:[28]

1. To promote the concept of alcoholism as a disease through education and identification.
2. To work to insure that appropriate agencies focus on early identification and case findings of drinking problems.
3. To work to insure that appropriate agencies focus on the early treatment and rehabilitation of persons with drinking problems and their families.
4. To increase public awareness and reduce the stigma of the disease of alcoholism.

The following list is a brief summary of the services provided by the NCA:

1. Personal, pre-treatment consultation by phone or in one of the council's local offices, for alcoholics, their families, friends, and business associates.
2. A twenty-four hour crisis line for persons in need of guidance and assistance for their own or another's alcohol use.
3. Public education programs, including films and speakers, for groups, as well as specialized programs and/or in-service training for members of the medical profession, clergy, teachers, and other concerned professionals.
4. Consultation to businesses, industry, unions, and govern-

ment agencies for the development of programs to deal effectively with the costly problem of employee alcoholism.

5. All services are confidential and provided without charge.

6. The San Francisco Bay Area Chapter also operates DWI (driving while intoxicated) school. This was established at the court's request in order to provide an educational experience for persons convicted of first-offense drunk driving.

The NCA feels that alcoholism is the most neglected problem in the United States.

## Alcoholics Anonymous, Al-Anon, Alateen

The most successful international, nonprofit organization helping individuals with drug and alcohol problems today is Alcoholics Anonymous. What is AA? Their credo is simply stated:

Alcoholics Anonymous is a fellowship of men and women who share their experience, strength, and hope with each other that they may so solve their common problem and help others to recover from alcoholism. The only requirement for membership is a desire to stop drinking. There are no dues or fees for AA membership; it is self-supporting through member contributions. AA is not allied with any sect, denomination, political organization, or institution; does not wish to engage in any controversy; neither endorses nor opposes any cause. Their primary purpose is to stay sober, and help other alcoholics to achieve sobriety.[29]

Alcoholics Anonymous, Al-Anon, and Alateen are all self-help groups: groups of people who have a family member, a friend, or are themselves afflicted with alcoholism. Al-Anon members are the adult relatives of alcoholics, whereas Alateen's members are the teenage relatives of an alcoholic. In each of these organizations, members are helped through the support and understanding of the group, and offered a simple twelve-step program to follow. These steps are designed to help evolve an understanding of the effects of alcoholism and how it has personally affected their lives. Emphasis is placed on sustaining the person's strengths and capabilities. AA is available every day of the week, and is open twenty-four hours a day.

Since the fellowship of AA was founded in 1935 it has grown from two members to over 1,000,000. There are now more than 48,000 groups and members located in 110 countries.

# How to Tell When Drinking is Becoming a Problem

Answer the following questions as honestly as you can.

|  | Yes | No |
|---|---|---|
| 1. Do you lose time from work due to drinking? | ☐ | ☐ |
| 2. Is drinking making your home life unhappy? | ☐ | ☐ |
| 3. Do you drink because you are shy with other people? | ☐ | ☐ |
| 4. Is drinking affecting your reputation? | ☐ | ☐ |
| 5. Have you ever felt remorse after drinking? | ☐ | ☐ |
| 6. Have you gotten into financial difficulties as a result of drinking? | ☐ | ☐ |
| 7. Do you turn to lower companions and an inferior environment when drinking? | ☐ | ☐ |
| 8. Does your drinking make you careless of your family's welfare? | ☐ | ☐ |
| 9. Has your ambition decreased since drinking? | ☐ | ☐ |
| 10. Do you crave a drink at a definite time daily? | ☐ | ☐ |
| 11. Do you want a drink the next morning? | ☐ | ☐ |
| 12. Does drinking cause you to have difficulty in sleeping? | ☐ | ☐ |
| 13. Has your efficiency decreased since drinking? | ☐ | ☐ |
| 14. Is drinking jeopardizing your job or business? | ☐ | ☐ |
| 15. Do you drink to escape from worries or trouble? | ☐ | ☐ |
| 16. Do you often drink alone, rather than with others? | ☐ | ☐ |
| 17. Have you ever had a complete loss of memory as a result of drinking? | ☐ | ☐ |
| 18. Has your physician ever treated you for drinking? | ☐ | ☐ |
| 19. Do you drink to build up your self-confidence? | ☐ | ☐ |
| 20. Have you ever been to a hospital or institution on account of drinking? | ☐ | ☐ |

If you have answered YES to any one of the questions, there is a definite warning that you **may be alcoholic.**

If you have answered YES to any two, the chances are that you **are an alcoholic.**

If you have answered YES to **three or more, you are definitely an alcoholic.**

(The above Test Questions are used by John Hopkins University Hospital, Baltimore, Md., in deciding whether or not a patient is alcoholic.)

# Chapter 9

# National Groups Influencing DUI Legislation

Three vital national groups have formed to arouse public awareness of the drunk driving problem. These groups are: Remove Intoxicated Drivers (RID), Mothers Against Drunk Drivers (MADD), and Students Against Driving Drunk (SADD).

## RID

RID was started in February, 1978, after two young people in Schenectady, N.Y. were killed by a drunk driver who went unpunished for his "crime." Realizing from this incident how lax the laws were on drunk driving, Doris Aiken, television show hostess, housewife, and mother of two from the same city, and a few friends set out to change the system. They gathered research on what happens to the drunk driver in our criminal justice system, asking why the drunk driver who has killed is not also jailed instead of being allowed to continue driving an automobile. Their research provided them with surprising statistics, including: the odds are two to one a person will be involved in an alcohol-related crash sometime in their life, and a person driving under the influence has an average blood alcohol of .19 percent. This means the average drunk driver consumes fifteen drinks during the two hours prior to driving. In fact, at the time RID was established, even after killing or maiming someone, most drivers were permitted to keep conditional licenses, work permits, and disability licenses; there were no absolute driver's license revocations.

Following this research, RID joined forces with Parkit, CCAD, and RAID from Ithaca, Syracuse, and Rochester, respectively, and helped to pass these laws:

1. An end to plea bargaining for drunk drivers.
2. Immediate license revocation for BAC test refusal.
3. Drunken driving was made a reckless *per se* charge.
4. An automatic felony charge for leaving the scene of a personal injury crash, as well as other loophole-closing measures.

According to Aiken, "People are voluntarily changing their drinking and driving habits." States that have instituted safety checkpoints have shown a decreased incidence of patronizing bars among younger people, who comprise twenty to forty percent of drinking drivers. New York tavern owners now complain that customers no longer "stop for four or five drinks before going home after work." During peak bar scene hours — 10 p.m. to 5 a.m. — fatalities have dropped twenty-two percent in New York alone. The bottom line is fewer deaths and injuries.

Public acceptance of safety checkpoints and tougher drunk driving laws rose considerably in 1983. A Harris poll indicated that seventy-six percent of those questioned nationally supported safety checkpoints. Over 3000 questionnaires completed by New York residents at the State Fair in 1983 showed that eighty-five percent favor checkpoints, ninety percent favor immediate license suspension for DUI, and ninety-eight percent felt that drunk driving is a serious problem.

According to RID, the most important factor in controlling drunk driving is citizen concern at the local level; keeping watch on the operations of the criminal justice system. RID feels weak laws will work if you strengthen the will of prosecutors and judges. RID's claims are many; a sampling of their accomplishments follows:

1. RID is a 100-percent volunteer endeavor, spending ninety-five percent of its income on programs and services for drunk driving victims and the community.

2. RID is funded by individual memberships and occasional memorial donations from families of victims. It does not solicit or accept funding from the alcohol industry.

3. Although RID is not prohibitionist, they *are* opposed to the excessive promotion of beer on college campuses and have joined with twenty-four other organizations in a petition

drive to remove radio and TV alcohol advertising aimed at youth.

4. RID fosters strong, autonomous, local citizen action groups rather than a centrally located national organization. Since RID's inception, forty-two states have reformed their drunk driving laws, fatalities due to drunk driving have dropped by 5,000 in the U.S. in one year, twenty-four states now have a drinking age of twenty-one, and, by 1986, RID believes that twenty-one will be the national drinking age standard for America.

5. RID is the oldest of the citizen action groups to initiate a citizen's revolt against drunk driving.

Currently, RID maintains a national twenty-four-hour hotline (518/372-0034) for victims of drunk drivers, as well as a network of helping hands throughout America.[30]

## MADD

Mothers Against Drunk Drivers (MADD) was started in 1980 by Candy Lightner of Sacramento after her teenage daughter was killed by a drunk driver who went unpunished for this slaying. Since the founding of MADD, Candy Lightner has become a national and international figure. MADD has influenced legislation to tighten up loopholes in drunk driving laws and is currently spearheading a national law that requires the minimum drinking age to be twenty-one. In December of 1983 a presidential commission, formed at the urging of MADD and several congressmen, recommended federal penalties for states that did not enact a minimum drinking age of twenty-one.[31]

MADD has 291 chapters in twenty-one states and over a half-million supporters. Lightner says, "We're seeing Fortune

500 companies providing taxi service for employees who've had too much to drink at office parties. We're seeing the National Restaurant Association recommending the elimination of happy hours that offer two drinks for the price of one. We're seeing car dealers against drunk drivers, truckers against drunk drivers. We're seeing police set up sobriety checkpoints. All of these measures would have been unpopular four years ago." MADD has lobbied strongly for "21" and it appears RID and MADD together will be accomplishing their goal of "21" as the national drinking age.

Lightner was honored by Civitan International, a civic organization that honors those who transform a personal tragedy into an effort to educate, inform, and change society in the best tradition of good citizenship. MADD was honored by the National Organization of Victim Assistance (NOVA), and by the Epilepsy Foundation of America. Lightner has become such an accomplished public speaker that she has been urged to run for political office.[32]

## SADD

A public outcry has arisen due to the efforts of these two pioneering groups. Many responsible groups are now taking a stand. Bartenders are even attending classes in how to handle persons needing to be stopped from drinking. As this public outcry reaches a high point, many new action groups are emerging. One segment of society most affected by drinking and driving is the sixteen-to-twenty-four-year-old group; from this group has emerged Students Against Driving Drunk (SADD). SADD was started in 1981 to improve young people's awareness, knowledge, and attitudes about alcohol and drugs. The program has three major components:

1. It provides a series of lesson plans to present the facts about drinking and driving which allows high school students to make informed decisions.

2. It mobilizes students to help one another, through peer pressure, to face up to the dangers of mixing driving with alcohol or drugs.

3. It promotes frank dialogue between teenagers and their parents through the SADD CONTRACT. Under this agreement, both students and their parents pledge to contact each other should they ever find themselves in a potential DUI situation (see Charts 8 and 9, pages 89–90).

**Chart 8**

# CONTRACT FOR LIFE

## A Contract for Life
## Between Parent and Teenager
### The SADD Drinking-Driver Contract

**Teenager**   I agree to call you for advice and/or transportation at any hour, from any place, if I am ever in a situation where I have been drinking or a friend or date who is driving me has been drinking.

_____
Signature

**Parent**   I agree to come and get you at any hour, any place, no questions asked and no argument at that time, or I will pay for a taxi to bring you home safely. I expect we would discuss this issue at a later time.

I agree to seek safe, sober transportation home if I am ever in a situation where I have had too much to drink or a friend who is driving me has had too much to drink.

_____
Signature

_____
Date

Distributed by SADD Students Against Driving Drunk

TM
1984

Permission for reprint granted by SADD.

# Chart 9

Dear Parents,

As an educator and a parent of three teenage boys, I understand
your concerns about the use and abuse of alcohol and other drugs by
our children. My experience has led me to believe that as determined
as we are to provide for our children a drug free environment;
statistics have proven that our efforts to date have fallen on deaf
ears.

This is not to say that we must not continue to work toward this
end, but must begin to react to the present reality. As our children
grow, it seems we become less and less a part of their intimate world.
We hear such things as; "Don't worry." "I know what I'm doing." "It's
my business." "My world is different from yours." No wonder many of
us are shocked when we find out that our children have been using
illegal substances.

I am convinced that parents and their children by working
together, and by recognizing how death has been camouflaged through
lack of communication can eliminate this needless slaughter on our
highways.

The SADD "Contract for Life" is meant to act as a safe guard
against death. I believe, that if our children realize that they can
and should call us if they are ever faced with a drinking - driving
situation; that this does not condone the illegal use of alcohol on
their part. It does, however, show that our love for our children and
their love for us is strong enough to combat any obstacle that may
force them to challenge death.

Our children are precious; believe in them, as they believe
in you.

Sincerely,

Robert Anastas
Founder & Executive Director

**FRIENDS DON'T LET FRIENDS DRIVE DRUNK**

SADD was founded by Robert Anastas, former director of Health Education for the Wayland Public School system in Wayland, Massachusetts. The original SADD program consisted of a mandatory high school course for sophomores on drinking and driving. Gradually it progressed to its current status as a national organization.[33]

One of the latest joint campaigns of MADD and SADD discourages the promotion of alcoholic beverages on college campuses. In an article by Candy Lightner published by the *Los Angeles Times* (May 6, 1984) she stated that colleges reported that eighty percent of vandalism on their campuses in 1982 was alcohol-related. Further, more than ninety percent of the deaths on campus are the results of hazing and involve heavy use of alcohol. And, according to the article, sixty percent of college failure was related to alcohol consumption and abuse.[34]

Colleges are reacting to this campaign by offering programs to promote safe and responsible drinking as an alternative to the campus "chug-a-lug" party. Many colleges, in conjunction with MADD, are observing Alcohol Awareness Week, which promotes healthful products, nonalcoholic bars, and programs in which sober students give others who have had too much to drink a ride home. MADD advocates banning alcohol on college campuses. They recommend that responsible drinking be encouraged by groups such as Boost Alcohol Consciousness Concerning the Health of University Students (BACCHUS) and SADD. MADD also advocates that treatment programs in college be offered, such as those developed by Alcoholics Anonymous.

According to the National Council on Alcoholism, there are well over 10,000,000 alcoholics in the United States. The majority of adults in the United States and the rest of the world use alcohol recreationally. This, unfortunately, turns to abuse for many drinkers. The situation is exacerbated as advertisers bombard the media and the young potential consumer.

The alcohol problem is immense and the outlook bleak; however, if two housewives from opposite ends of the country can have such an impact on our laws and our consciousness, the future is hopeful.

Chapter 10

# How to Send Your Guests Home Sober

The following suggestions were presented by RID president Doris Aiken and James M. Schaefer, Director of the Office of Alcohol and Other Drug-abuse Programs at the University of Minnesota.[35]

1. Plan your event carefully; estimate how much alcohol to have on hand based on the number of guests and the length of the party (one drink per guest) and limit the amount of liquor you purchase in the first place.

2. Have guests throw their car keys in a big punch bowl when they arrive. Return the keys at evening's end, when each driver is clearly capable of operating a car.

3. Suggest the concept of the "designated driver." One person is selected in advance to be the driver for the evening. That person agrees not to drink.

4. Provide a theme or organize social events throughout the evening so that guests do not break into segregated huddles of heavy drinkers/nondrinkers.

5. Regard alcohol as the highly toxic substance it is; know its effects. And most important, be aware of how much to consume.

6. Know the law in your state and follow it. At parties attended by young people, be conscious of the drinking age and remember that serving minors is illegal.

7. Provide attractive, nonalcoholic drinks as a matter of course (see list on pages 96 and 97).

8. Avoid carbonated mixers; use noncarbonated mixers (such as fruit juice). Carbonation speeds alcohol absorption.

9. Provide nutritious, attractively presented foods throughout the evening to help slow absorption of alcohol into the bloodstream.

10. Avoid having an open bar and be certain to measure all drinks. Enjoy, savor, and sip, but treat alcohol as a drug.

11. Don't push guests to drink. One drink per hour is about all the body can safely absorb and eliminate. Let guests ask for refills.

12. Avoid serving after-dinner drinks (substitute coffee or other nonalcoholic beverages). Cut off drinks at least one hour before a party ends.

13. Recognize that drunkenness is neither healthy, humorous, nor safe. Don't excuse otherwise unacceptable behavior just because someone had "too much to drink."

14. If, in spite of precautions, your guests are impaired, assume responsibility for their safety. Consider driving them home yourself, calling a taxi, or encourage them to stay over night.

15. Always have a list of telephone numbers on hand for emergency health care, police, or taxis.

# Nonalcoholic Drink Recipe Books

### Drinks for Driving: Nonalcoholic

1983    33 pages    $1.00
Pillsbury Company Publishers
Available from:    Prevention Resource Center
2829 Verndale Avenue
Anoka, MN 55303
(612) 427-5310

### Nondrinker's Drink Book

Gail Schioler    1981    158 pages    $8.95
Personal Library, Toronto    ISBN# 0-920510-80-9
Available from:    Dodd, Mead & Company
77 Madison Avenue
New York, NY 10016

### A Toast to Sober Spirits & Joyous Juices

Jan Blexrud    1976    100 pages    $6.95
CompCare Publications    ISBN# 0-89638-012-2
Available from:    CompCare Publications
2419 North Annapolis Lane
Plymouth, MN 55441
(612) 559-4800

# Nonalcoholic Beers

| | |
|---|---|
| Apple Beer | Beverage Canners<br>P.O. Box 680280<br>Miami, FL 33168 |
| Apple Beer | Apple Beer Corporation<br>Salt Lake City, UT 84125 |
| Birell Beer | Swiss Gold A.G.<br>(Schmidt Brewery)<br>Philadelphia, PA 19123 |
| Texas Select Beer | Richland Corporation<br>P.O. Box 58024<br>Dallas, TX 75258 |
| Schmidt Select Beer | G. Heileman Brewing Co., Inc.<br>882 West 7th Street<br>St. Paul, MN 55105 |
| Schlitz, Schafer, Malta | The Stroh Brewery Company<br>One Stroh Drive<br>Detroit, MI 43226 |
| Moussy Beer | White Rock Products Corporation<br>New York, NY 11357 |

Goetz Pale Near Beer

Kingsbury Brew Near Beer

Pearl Brewing Company
San Antonio, TX

G. Heileman Brewing Co., Inc.
882 West 7th Street
St. Paul, MN 55105

# Nonalcoholic Wines

Meiers
Pink Sparkling Catawba Juice
Sparkling Catawba Juice
Pink Catawba Grape Juice
Catawba Grape Juice
Cold Duck
Sparkling DeChannac Grape Juice
Sparkling Burgundy Grape Juice
Sparkling Apple Cider

Distributed by:
Gourmet Foods, Inc.
860 Vandalia Street
St. Paul, MN 55114

Welches
Sparkling Red Grape Juice
Sparking White Grape Juice

The Food Service
Welch Foods Inc.
Westfield, NY

Martinelli's Sparkling Cider

Gourmet Foods
860 Vandalia Street
St. Paul, MN 55114

Sparkling Apple
Sparkling Grape

Hudson Valley Wines
Blue Point Road
Highland, NY 12528

Felton Empire
Dealcoholized Wine

Felton Empire
379 Felton Empire Road
Felton, CA 95018

Wollersheim
Sparkling Apple Juice
Sparkling Niagara Grape Juice
Sparkling Concord Grape Juice

Wollersheim Winery
Prairie du Sac, WI

Alive Polarity Grape Juice

The Alive Fellowship
Murrieta Hot Springs
Murrieta, CA 92362

Carl Jung
Weisslack
Rotlack
Roselack
Boosenberg Mousseaux

Alternative Beverage
Distributors
511 11th Avenue South
Minneapolis, MN 55415

Giovane

Alternative Beverage
Distributors
511 11th Avenue South
Minneapolis, MN 55415

# Chapter 11

---

# How You Can Make a Difference in Your Community

Drunk driving is a community disaster. John Moulten, NHTSA psychologist, calls it, "A prime cause for that old civic duty stuff; this is literally one of our number one health and safety issues." [36] RID president Doris Aiken suggests the following nine ways you can make a difference:

1. Join RID, start a RID chapter, or work as a victim-support volunteer. The latter is a national network of people who have agreed to help victims in their area by researching the driver's record, contacting media, and working with the district attorney to assure that every offender is brought to justice. These volunteers needn't actually join a RID chapter. RID emphasizes local chapter autonomy; chapters set their own dues and agendas. They work toward individual legislative goals. It costs $30.00 to start a RID chapter and $10.00 to receive the monthly newsletter. Write to: P.O. Box 520, Schenectady, New York, 12301.[37]

2. Join MADD. This organization does essentially the same thing as RID, but with a greater national emphasis. The national MADD staff in Hurst, Texas provides chapters with regional workshops, newsletters, and access to national victim counselors and legislative resources. There is heavy emphasis on raising national awareness. MADD and RID often trade volunteers when one group is asked for assistance in a town where the other group already has a chapter. MADD's goals include establishing a uniform legal drinking age of twenty-one and increased public awareness of the drunk driving problem, both here and abroad. Individual membership is $20, senior citizen membership is $10, family membership is $40, and the fee is $150 or more for an organization to become an affiliate. Write to: 669 Airport Freeway, Suite 310, Hurst, Texas, 76053.[38]

3. Join a county task force or citizen advisory committee. County task forces are an effective way for communities to assess the problem in their backyards. The idea is to bring together judges, police, MADD, RID, prosecutors, parole officers, treatment services, public information channels, school administrators, alcohol retailers, or any-

one else with a role in the drama to explore solutions. In every state there is a governor's highway safety representative who monitors anti-DUI efforts for the county. You may be able to join your county task force or help organize one.

4. Act through civic, social, or fraternal ties. You do not need to join a new organization to speak out against drunk driving. If you belong to a fraternal organization there may be a liquor bar on your club premises. Initiate an awareness program for the benefit of your peers, or for the public you serve.

5. Join SADD. Local SADD chapters can be established in high schools throughout the nation at a relatively modest cost. First contact the national SADD organization for assistance in scheduling an organizational meeting. Invite students, faculty, and parent representatives from surrounding high schools to attend the organizational session. Speakers from your governor's office, the Department of Education, and the insurance industry should also appear. The director of SADD, Mr. Anastas, and other representatives, are available on a limited basis to visit your community. They need about two month's lead time for scheduling. Write to: Mr. Robert Anastas, Students Against Driving Drunk, P.O. Box 800, Marlboro, Massachusetts, 017852.[39]

6. Report suspected drunk drivers. Law enforcement officials need your help. A free guide is available from any state police installation which includes these clues to a suspected drunk driver: [40]

(a) Exaggerated, erratic driving patterns.

(b) Ignoring, overshooting, or hanging back at stop signs or traffic lights.

(c) Unusually fast or slow driving, possibly alternating fast/slow speeds.

(d) Driving too close to the edge of the road or straddling the center line.

(e) Frequent and sudden lane changing or passing without sufficient clearance or signals.

(f) Driving at night without lights, failing to dim lights to oncoming traffic, or driving with the interior dome light on and/or headlights off.

(g) Driving with windows down in cold weather or driving with the head part way out of the window.

7. For those with CB radios, here are some useful tips for giving an Impaired Driver Alert (IDA):

(a) Get on channel nine (the police channel) and say, "Emergency, any base station. Impaired driver alert." Pause and wait briefly for police REACT monitor to acknowledge.

(b) You may get no reply; remember, monitors can hear you when you can't hear them . . . and they can act. After a pause, proceed to describe the incident.

(c) Give the exact location (identify road and direction) of vehicle, including model, color, license plate number, etc. DO NOT say the driver is "drunk," describe only the manner in which the vehicle is being operated.

(d) Identify your station so the monitor can call you back.

(e) Stand by once again for acknowledgement or questions, then repeat the entire IDA; monitors often need to hear it several times.

(f) DO NOT attempt to become personally involved with the vehicle or driver being reported.

(g) Remember, channel nine is for emergencies and traveler's assistance only. Do not use channel nine for other CB radio communication.

8. Write one letter, make one call. If you do nothing more than this, these two overt actions can help change the way negligent homicide has been viewed for years in your community. This is the opinion of most expert activists. Aiken describes her experiences as being a "court hawk." They have taught her that drunk driving is definitely an issue where a single individual can make a difference. So write a local judge and spell out your concerns, asking that your letter be made part of the public record. Or call the district attorney and ask his/her policy on drunk driving, letting him or her know you consider it a major crime. Explain your intention to look over his or her shoulder in the future to observe DUI policy and performance.

9. *Rethink your attitudes.* Ten years ago, nonsmoking sections in restaurants and airplanes were an oddity. Today they are considered a social right. Drunk driving experts hope the nondrinking option will eventually achieve similar status. The University of Minnesota's Office of Alcohol and Other Drug-abuse Programs, directed by James M. Schaefer, has collected data on over 300 available nonalcoholic drinks. These include near-beer, dealcoholized wines, nonalcoholic champagnes, mixed drink substitutes, mineral waters, and soft drinks. Many of these drinks are becoming a status symbol on the cocktail circuit. According to Schaefer, "Much ritual is laid on people to drink. But now nonalcoholic drinks are being served with as

much flair as the alcoholic ones; there's been a real attitude change recently." Other examples of this change include alternative lounges which serve no liquor at all and traditional taverns that provide taxi service for intoxicated patrons.

Forty percent of Americans in a recent Gallup poll admitted to having driven after drinking. What about you? Do you excuse the peer or spouse who gets drunk and takes the wheel? We as a nation have to change our human behavior and integrate the idea that getting drunk and driving is socially unacceptable and dangerous to our health and to others.[41] *If we take others into consideration as part of our everyday awareness, we will be contributing to a safer community and world.*

# Appendix A

## Driving Under the Influence Laws in the United States

Permission for reprint granted by National Safety Council.

# ALABAMA

<u>1984 Legislation:</u>
None passed.

Per Se: .10
Drinking Age: 19 yrs.
Dram Shop Law: Yes, §6-5-90.
Open Container Prohibition: None.
Section 408 Grant: Received $556,418 Alcohol/Traffic Safety Grant (Basic only). In order to qualify for Supplemental Incentive Grant, state must revoke lic. within 45 days of arrest, or within 90 days of arrest and submit plan to reduce it to 45 days.)

Refusals to Submit (admissible):
    1st refusal: 30 days hard lic. revoc., 60 days restricted.
    2nd refusal: 1 yr. lic. revoc.
    If acquitted of criminal DUI, revoc. may be reduced.

Driving under Revoc. License:
    Misdemeanor, $100-500, 180 days jail. Additional 6 mos. lic. revoc.

| | Penalties | Jail/CommSvc | LicRevoc/Rehab/Therapy | Other |
|---|---|---|---|---|
| 1st Offense | $250-500, | | 30 days hard lic. revoc., 60 days restricted revoc. Rehab. | |
| 2nd Offense w/in 5 yrs. | $500-2500, | Mand. 48 hrs.-1 yr. jail or 20 days comm. svc. | 1 yr. lic. revoc. | |
| 3rd Offense w/in 5 yrs. | $1000-5000, | Mand. 60 days-1 yr. jail, | 3 yrs. lic. revoc. | |
| Homicide by m.v. | $500-2000, | 1-5 yrs. jail. | | |

# ALASKA

<u>1984 Legislation:</u>
Nothing passed.

Per Se: .10
Drinking Age: 21 yrs.
Dram Shop Law: Applies to businesses only (not private hosts) and only if the person served was already intoxicated.
Open Container Prohibition: None.
Section 408 Grant: Received $262,000 Alcohol/Traffic Safety Grant (Basic and Supplemental).
PBTs: Allowed, refusal is admissible in court.

Refusals to Submit, or if .10 BAC:
    Same penalties as for criminal offenses (see below). Lic. revoc. are administratively imposed and all hard revocs. (no restricted lic. avail.). Lic. revocs. for DWI and refusal/.10 BAC admin. can run either consecutively or concurrently.

Driving under DWI Revoc. License:
  1st Offense: Min. $500, mand. 30 days jail.
  2nd Offense: Min. $1000, mand. 90 days jail.

|  | Penalties | Jail/CommSvc | LicRevoc/Rehab/Therapy | Other |
|---|---|---|---|---|
| 1st Offense | Min. $250, | Mand. 72 consecutive hrs. jail, | 30 days hard. admin. lic. revoc., 60 days restricted admin. lic. revoc., rehab. | |
| 2nd Offense w/in 10 yrs. | Min. $500, | Mand. 20 consecutive days jail, | 1 yr. hard admin. lic. revoc., rehab. | Possible vehicle impoundment. |
| 3rd Offense w/in 10 yrs. | Min. $1000, | Mand. 30 days jail, | 10 yrs. hard admin. lic. revoc., rehab. | Possible vehicle impoundment. |

Miscellaneous:
  Cannot refuse BAC if death/physical injury occured.

## ARIZONA

### 1984 Legislation:

HB2307 (ch.257) - Clarifies that if blood is taken from a "refuser" for any reason, police have right to a sample. Info on prior convictions/pending charges are admissible (at court's discretion) any time prior to start of trial. New punishment for DWI and driving without lic. Mand. 6 mos. jail before any parole/probation can be offered.

HB2027 (ch.2) - Deletes provision for 1st offenders allowing probation and only fine instead of other penalties.

HB2149 (Ch.67) - Raised legal drinking age from 19 to 21 yrs. old. Provides 2 yr. lic. revoc. if underage DWI, or if 2nd offense of underage possession.

Per Se: .10
Drinking Age: 21 yrs. (new)
Dram Shop Law: No statute, and case law does not appear to support such 3rd party liability in absence of statute.
Open Container Prohibition: Partial; illegal to drink while driving.
Section 408 Grant: Received $701,413 Alcohol/Traffic Safety Grant (Basic and Supplemental).

Refusals to Submit:
  1 yr. admin. lic. revoc., admissible as evidence.

Driving under Revoc. License:
  Class 1 misdemeanor, mand. 48 hrs. jail, double original lic. revoc.

|  | Penalties | Jail/CommSvc | LicRevoc/Rehab/Therapy | Other |
|---|---|---|---|---|
| 1st Offense | Class 1 misdemeanor, Mand $250 | Mand. 24 hrs. jail. 8-24 hrs. comm. svc. | Mand. 90 days lic. revoc., rehab. | OR probation, same penalties except no rehab. or comm. svc. |

| | | | | |
|---|---|---|---|---|
| 1st Offense if BAC less than .20 and no injury | Mand. $250. | 8-24 hrs. comm. svc. | Rehab. 30 days hard lic. revoc, 60 days restricted. | OR probation, but same penalties (new). |
| 2nd Offense w/in 5 yrs | Class 1 misdemeanor, mand. $500 | Mand. 60 days jail | Mand. 1 yr. hard lic. revoc., rehab. | OR probation but same penalties. |
| 3rd Offense w/in 5 yrs | Class 5 felony | Mand. 6 mos. jail | Mand. 3 yrs. lic. revoc., rehab. | |

Miscellaneous:
Jurisdictions may establish **minimum security facilities for drunk driving** jail terms of less than 180 days.

## ARKANSAS

1984 Legislation:
None; did not meet.

Per Se: .10
Drinking Age: 21 yrs.
Dram Shop Law: none
Open Container Prohibition: none

Refusals to Submit (not strictly administrative, lic. pulled, but temporary lic. issued until trial.):
1st refusal: 6 mos. lic. revoc.
2nd refusal w/in 3 yrs.: 1 yr. lic. revoc.

Driving under Revoc. License:
10 days jail, 90 days vehicle impoundment.

| | Penalties | Jail/CommSvc | LicRevoc/Rehab/Therapy | Other |
|---|---|---|---|---|
| 1st Offense | Misdemeanor, $150-1000. | 24 hrs.-1 yr. jail or comm. svc. | Min. 90 day lic. revoc., pre-sentencing assessment. Rehab or probation (no expungement of record). | |
| 2nd Offense w/in 3 yrs. | $400-3000, | 7 days-3 yrs. jail. | Min. 1 yr. lic. revoc., pre-sentencing assessment. Rehab. | |
| 3rd Offense w/in 3 yrs. | $900-5000, | 90 days-1 yr. jail. | Min. 2 yr. lic. revoc., pre sentencing assessment. Rehab. | |
| 4th Offense | Felony, $900-5000, | 1-6 yrs. jail. | Min. 3 yr. lic. revoc., pre-sentencing assessment. Rehab. | |

## CALIFORNIA

<u>1984 Legislation:</u>
<u>SB1441 (CH.326)</u> - Increases lic. revoc. to 3 yrs. for refusal after 2 prior offenses.

<u>SB1411</u> (not yet signed by Governor) - Provides for lic. revoc. for minors who commit any DWI offense (even where lic. revoc. is not part of existing penalties such as open container violation).

Bills pending, but expected to pass (session ends August 31, 1984, all have passed originting House):
<u>SB1522</u> - Relates to vehicle impoundment for 2nd and 3rd offenders.

<u>AB3834</u> - DWI misdemeanor does not have to occur in presence of police officer (as other misdemeanors need to be). Example: Intoxicated driver in car on road, but not driving can be charged with DWI.

<u>AB3832</u> - Technical change relating to prior offenses considered separate offenses.

<u>AB3509</u> - Statutorily mandates no drinking and driving as one term of probation. DMV records to show driver on probation. Requires probation agreement to inlcude mand. 2 days jail if BAC .04 while on probation. Requires all plea bargained to "wet-reckless charge" to be considered as alcohol-offenses for purposes of DWI sentence enhancement.

Per Se: .10
Drinking Age: 21 yrs.
Dram Shop Law: Liability specifically forbidden by statute although it is illegal to sell to intoxicated person; BP§25602.
Open Container Prohibition: Exists.

Refusals to Submit:
    1st refusal: 6 mos. admin. lic. revoc.
    2nd refusal: 1 yr. lic. revoc.
    3rd refusal: 3 yr. lic. revoc. (new)
    If hearing requested, revoc. stayed pending outcome.
    Defendent has choice of tests. If choose breath, police can require blood/urine for drug detection.

Driving under DWI Revoc. License:
    1st Offense: Max. $500, 10 days-6 mos. jail, or probation, 10 days jail.
    2nd Offense: Max. $1000, 30 days-1 yr. jail, or probation, maxx. 30 days jail.

Youth Offender Legislation:
    If convicted of DWI, lic. revoked until 18th birthday, 1 yr. or peeriod specified in statute, whichever is longest.

| | Penalties | Jail/CommSvc | LicRevoc/Rehab/Therapy | Other |
|---|---|---|---|---|
| 1st Offense, no injury | $390-500, | 96 hrs.-6 mos. jail, | 6 mos. lic. revoc. | |
| If probation, | $390-5000, | 48 hrs.-6 mos. jail, | 6 mos. lic. revoc. | |
| OR | $390-500, . | | 90 days restricted lic. | |

| | Penalties | Jail/CommSvc | LicRevoc/Rehab/Therapy | Other |
|---|---|---|---|---|
| 2nd offense w/in 5 yrs., no injury | $375-1000, | 90 days-1 yr. jail, | 1 yr. lic. revoc. | |
| If probation | $390-1000, | 10 days-1 yr. jail, | 1 yr. lic. revoc. | |
| OR | $390-1000, | 48 hrs.-1 yr. jail, | 1 yr. hard lic. revoc., 2 yrs. restricted, 1 yr. rehab. | |
| 3rd Offense w/in 5 yrs., injury | $390-1000, | 120 days-1 yr. jail, | 3 yrs. lic. revoc. | |
| If probation | $390-1000, | 120 days-1 yr. jail, | 3 yrs lic. revoc., 1 yr. rehab. | |
| 4th Offense w/in 5 yrs., no injury | $390-1000, | 180 days jail, | 4 yrs. lic. revoc. | |
| If probation | Same. | | | |
| 1st offense, injury occured | $390-5000, | 90 days-1 yr. jail, | 1 yr. lic. revoc., rehab. | |
| If probation | $390-1000, | 5 days-1 yr. jail, | 1 yr. lic. revoc., rehab. | |
| 2nd Offense w/in 5 yrs., injury occured | $390-5000, | 120 days-1 yr. jail, | 3 yrs. lic. revoc. | |
| If probation | $390-1000, | Min. 120 days jail, | 3 yrs. lic. revoc. | |
| OR | $390-1000, | 30 days-1 yr. jail, | 1 yr. hard lic. revoc., 2 yrs. restricted lic. revoc., 1 yr. rehab. | |
| 3rd Offense w/in 5 yrs., injury occured | $1015-5000, | 2-4 yrs. jail, | 5 yrs. lic. revoc. | |
| If probation | $390-5000, | Min. 1 yr. jail, | 5 yrs. lic. revoc., 1 yr. rehab. | Restitution |
| Vehicular Manslaughter while DWI & gross negligence | | 4-8 yrs. jail | | |
| Vehicular Manslaughter while DWI & not gross negligence | | 16 mos.-4 yrs. jail. | | |

* All penalties min. mand. unless noted.

Possible 1-30 day vehicle impoundments added to above penalties. Judge may order pre-sentence evaluation. Limits on plea bargains, info. must be recorded.

Miscellaneous:
   Probation Officer to notify victims of all sentencing proceedings and also give info. on victim's right to civil recovery and opportunity for compensation from Restitution Fund.

# COLORADO

**1984 Legislation:**
    HB1249 - Allows use of PBTs. Not admissible as evidence.

Per Se: .15
Drinking Age: 18 yrs. for 3.2 beer, 21 yrs. for everything else.
Dram Shop Law: Only if previous written notification not to serve individual is given (13-21-103).
Open Container Prohibition: None.
PBTs: See HB1249.

Refusals to Submit:
    Mand. 1 yr admin. lic. revoc., runs consecutively with criminal disposition.

.15 BAC:
    Mand. 1 yr. lic. revoc., if then convicted on criminal charges, lic. revoc. periods run
    concurrently.

Driving under Revoc. License:
    1st Offense:  Misdemeanor, $500-1000, mand. 30 days-1 yr. jail.
    2nd Offense:  $500-3000, mand. 90 days-2 yrs. jail, 4 yr. lic. revoc.

|  | Penalties | Jail/CommSvc | LicRevoc/Rehab/Therapy | Other |
|---|---|---|---|---|
| 1st Offense DWI (.15) | $300-1000 | Mand. 5 days-1 yr. jail or rehab. Mand 48-96 hrs. comm. svc. | No specific lic. revoc. period, court has option if public safety in danger. | |
| 2nd Offense DWI w/in 5 yrs | $500-1500 | Mand. 90 days-1 yr. jail or 7 days jail and rehab. Mand. 60-120 hrs. comm. svc. | Mand. lic. revoc. (generally until rehab completed). | |
| 1st Offense DWI w/in 5 yrs of 1st offense DWAI (below .15) | $450-1500 | Mand. 70 days-1 yr. jail. OR 7 days jail and rehab. Mand. 56-112 hrs. comm. svc. | Rehab. | |
| 1st Offense DWAI (below .15) | $100-500 | Mand. 2-180 days jail or rehab and 24-48 hrs. comm. svc. | No specific lic. revoc. except mand. 1 yr. for provisional licenses | OR probation, no mand. sentence if complete rehab. |

| | Penalties | Jail/CommSvc | LicRevoc/Rehab/Therapy | Other |
|---|---|---|---|---|
| 2nd offense DWAI (below .15 BAC) w/in 5 yrs. | $300-1000 | Mand. 45 days-1 yr. jail. OR 5 days jail and rehab. incl. 1 yr abstinence from alcohol. Mand. 48-96 hrs. comm. svc. | No specific lic. revoc. period. | |
| 1st offense DWAI w/in 5 yrs of 1st offense DWI | $400-1200 | Mand. 60 days-1 yr. jail. OR 6 days jail and rehab. Mand. 52-104 hrs. comm. svc. | Mand. lic.. revoc. | |
| 3rd Offense (any combination) | Habitual offender, $400-1200, | Mand. 60 days-1 yr. jail. OR 6 days jail and rehab. Mand. 52-104 hrs. comm. svc. | Min. mand. 2 yr. lic. revoc. | |
| Vehicular Homicide | Class 4 felony | | Mand. lic. revoc. | |
| Vehicular Assault | Class 5 felony | | Mand. lic. revoc. | |

Miscellaneous:
    Additional $50-60 assessment to fund Alcohol and Drug Driving Safety Program.
    Victims eligible for Crime Victim Compensation Program.

# CONNECTICUT

1984 Legislation:
    Nothing passed.

Per Se: .10 per se, .07-.10 Driving While Ability is Impaired (infraction).
Drinking Age: 20 yrs. If age in question, form must be filled out by purchaser. If misrepresent, $100-250.
Dram Shop Law: Maximum $20,000 per person injured, max. $50,000 per incident. Notice must be given to 3rd party within 60 days (Ch.545§30-102 [1935]).
Open Container Prohibition: No law, except there is prohibition against drinking and driving.

Refusals to Submit:
    1st refusal: 24 hr. lic. revoc. on spot + 6 mos. admin. lic. revoc.
    2nd refusal: 24 hr. lic. revoc. on spot + 1 yr. admin. lic. revoc.
    3rd refusal: 24 hr. lic. revoc. on spot + 3 yrs. admin. lic. revoc.

Driving under Revoc. License:
    $500-1000, mand. 5 days-1 yr. jail.

.10 BAC Administrative License Revocation:
    24 hrs.

Youth Offender Legislation:
    If DWI and under 18 yrs old, lic. revoc. until 18 yrs, or as set forth in penalty section, whichever
    is longer.

| | Penalties | Jail/CommSvc | LicRevoc/Rehab/Therapy | Other |
|---|---|---|---|---|
| 1st Offense | $500-1000. | Max. 6 mos. jail. | 1 yr. lic. revoc., rehab. | OR pre-trial alcohol educ., $250, 8 rehab. sessions, lic. revoc. during rehab. Upon completion, charges are dismissed, but record of participation given to DMV. |
| 2nd Offense | $500-2000. | Mand. 48 hrs.-1 yr. jail | 2 yrs. lic. revoc., rehab. | |
| 3rd Offense | $1000-4000 | Mand. 30 days-2 yrs. jail | 3 yrs. lic. revoc., rehab. | |
| 4th Offense | $2000-8000 | Mand. 1-3 yrs. jail. | Permanent lic. revoc., rehab. | |
| Assault-2nd degree w/m.v. | Class D felony, $5000 | Max. 5 yrs jail. | 1 yr. lic. revoc. | |
| Manslaughter-2nd degree w/ m.v. | Class C felony, $5000. | Max. 10 yrs. jail. | 1 yr. lic. revoc. | |

Miscellaneous:
    Plea bargaining to non-alcohol offense prohibited if BAC is .10+.


## DELAWARE

1984 Legislation:
    None.

Per Se: .10
Drinking Age: 21 yrs.
Dram Shop Law: No specific statute, but illegal to sell to intoxicated person. Case law available to
                support liability of vender under this statute.
Open Container Prohibition: None.
Section 408 Grant: Received $262,000 Alcohol/Traffic Safety Grant (Basic and Supplemental).
PBTs: Allowed.

Refusals to Submit (administratively imposed, admissible as evidence):
    1st refusal: 1 yr. hard. lic. revoc., rehab.
    2nd refusal: 18 mos. hard lic. revoc., rehab.
    3rd refusal: 24 mos. hard lic. revoc., rehab.

.10 BAC Administrative Penalties (separate from crim. disposition):
    1st Offense: Mand. 3 mos. lic. revoc.
    2nd Offense: Mand. 1 yr. lic. revoc.
    3rd Offense: Mand. 18 mos. lic. revoc.

## Drinking and Driving

Driving under DWI Revoc. License:
1st Offense: Mand $200-500, 30 days-6 mos. jail. Min. 90 day vehicle impoundment.
2nd Offense: Mand. $500-1000, mand. 60 days-1 yr. jail. Min. 1 yr. vehicle impoundment.

| | Penalties | Jail/CommSvc | LicRevoc/Rehab/Therapy | Other |
|---|---|---|---|---|
| 1st Offense | Mand. $200-1000 | &/OR 60 days-6 mos. jail. | 1 yr. lic. revoc., additional 6 mos. lic. revoc. or rehab. | |
| 1st Offense if BAC less than .20 and no injury Pre-trial diversion program | | | Mand. 1 yr. lic. revoc., work restricted lic. avail. after 16 hrs. rehab and 90 days lic. revoc. have elapsed. | |
| 2nd Offense w/in 5 yrs. | Mand. $500-2000 | Mand. 60 days-18 mos. jail. | Mand. 1 yr. lic. revoc., additional 6 mos. revoc. or rehab. | |
| 3rd Offense w/in 5 yrs | Mand. $500-2000 | Mand. 60 days-18 mos. jail | Mand. 18 mos. lic. revoc., additional 6 mos. revoc. or rehab. | |

## FLORIDA

1984 Legislation:
HB360 (ch 84-359) - Allows out-of-state convictions to be used when determining prior offenses.
Allows comm. svc. in lieu of fine if defendent financially unable. Youth offender leg.: if lic.
used to misrepresent age, can revoke lic. for 1 yr. and order max. 40 hrs. comm. svc.

Per Se: .10
Drinking Age: 19 yrs. (Bill to raise to 21 yrs. failed.)
Dram Shop Law: No dram shop law, but it is illegal to furnish to habitual drunkard if written notice has
              been given by immediate family.
Open Container Prohibition: None.
PBTs: Used, refusal not admissible.

Refusals to Submit (admissible as evidence):
1st refusal: 6 mos. lic. revoc.
2nd refusal: 1 yr. lic. revoc.

Driving under Revoc. License:
1st Offense: 2nd degree misdemeanor, $500, 60 days jail.
2nd Offense: 1st degree misdemeanor, $1000, 1 yr. jail.

| | Penalties | Jail/CommSvc | LicRevoc/Rehab/Therapy | Other |
|---|---|---|---|---|
| 1st Offense | $250-500. | Max. 6 mos. jail. Mand. 50 hrs. comm. svc. | 180 days-1 yr. lic revoc. Rehab. Work-restricted lic. avail. upon completion of rehab. | Mand. 1 yr. probation. |

114

| 2nd Offense w/in 3 yrs. | $500-1000. | Mand. 10 days-9 mos. jail. | Min. 5 yrs. lic. revoc. (if 2nd offense w/in 5 yrs), no work-restricted lic. avail. Rehab. | |
|---|---|---|---|---|
| 3rd Offense w/in 5 yrs. | Habitual offender, $1000-2500. | Mand. 30 days-12 mos. jail. | Min. 10 yrs. hard lic. revoc. (if 3rd offense w/in 10 yrs.). Rehab. | |
| DWI/serious bodily injury/ property damage | $1000, | OR max. 1 yr. jail, | | OR above penalties, whichever is tougher. |
| Vehicular homicide | 3rd degree felony, max. $5000 | max. 5 yrs. jail. | | |

## GEORGIA

1984 Legislation:
  SB61 - Restricts court from changing sentence after judgement is rendered.

  SB426 - Technical change

  SR362 - Resolution establishing Problem Drinker and Highway Safety Study Committee.

  HB1200 - DMV will suspend GA drivers' lic. for DWI conviction in another state.

Per Se: .12
Drinking Age: 19 yrs. (bill to raise to 21 yrs. failed in 2nd House in 1984).
Dram Shop Law: Limited to parents' right of action against person furnishing alcohol to their minor
    children.
Open Container Prohibition: None.

Refusals to Submit:
  12 mos. hard admin. lic. revoc., admissible as evidence.

Driving under Revoc. License:
  $500, 2 days-6 mos. jail, additional 1 yr. lic. revoc.

Driving under Revoked License and Habitual Offender:
  $750, 1-5 yrs. jail.

Youth Offender Legislation:
  If under 18 yrs. old, must complete 6 hr. drug/alcohol course before obtaining lic.

| | Penalties | Jail/CommSvc | LicRevoc/Rehab/Therapy | Other |
|---|---|---|---|---|
| 1st Offense | Mand. $300-$1000 | 10 days-1 yr jail | Mand. 1 yr. lic. revoc. OR 120 days +ASAP + $25. Work-restricted lic. avail. | OR plead no contest, rehab, no lic. revoc. |

115

| 2nd Offense w/in 5 yrs. | Mand. $600-1000 | Mand. 48 hrs.-1 yr. jail or 10 days comm. svc. | Mand. 3 yrs. lic. revoc. OR 120 days + ASAP + $25. Work-restricted lic. avail. | |
|---|---|---|---|---|
| 3rd Offense | Habitual offender, mand. $1000 | Mand. 10 days-1 yr. jail or 30 days comm. svc. | Indefinite lic. revoc. | |
| Homicide by m.v. while DWI | 1st degree homicide | 2-15 yrs. jail | Mand. 3 yr. hard lic. revoc. | |
| Habitual Offender DWI and homicide by m.v. | 1st degree homicide | 3-15 yrs. jail | | |

## HAWAII

### 1984 Legislation:

HB1629 - Sets up procedures for police to conduct roadblocks. All vehicles or vehicles in specific numbered sequence to be stopped. Uniformed police officers in sufficient quantity to assure speedy compliance. Minimum safety precautions must be met.

HB2103 - Establishments selling liquor must post DWI penalties.

HB2142 - Revisions to qualify for Sec. 408 grant. Provides assessment for 2nd and 3rd offenders with cost of treatment to be paid for by defendent.

HB2163 - Relating to penalties for adults allowing possession of alcohol by minors. Not illegal if alcohol is ingredient in medicine, used for religious ceremony, provided with consent of parent and belief that minor would not consume it or only consume it in presence of parent/legal guardian.

Per Se: .10
Drinking Age: 18 yrs.
Dram Shop Law: None.
Open Container Prohibition: Repealed 1971.

Refusals to Submit:
    $25-1000, 12 mos. lic. revoc.

Driving under Revoc. License:
    $250-1000, 1 yr. jail.

| | Penalties | Jail/CommSvc | LicRevoc/Rehab/Therapy | Other |
|---|---|---|---|---|
| 1st Offense w/in 5 yrs. | ONE OR MORE OF: $1000, 48 hrs. jail, 72 hrs. comm. svc. | | 14 hr. rehab., 30 days hard lic. revoc., 60 days restricted lic. revoc. | |
| 2nd Offense w/in 5 yrs. | $500-1000 | 48 hrs. jail or 80 hrs. comm. svc. | 1 yr. hard lic. revoc. Assessment, rehab (costs to be borne by defendent). | |
| 3rd Offense w/in 5 yrs. | $500-1000 | 10-180 days jail | 1-5 yrs. lic. revoc.. Assessment, rehab (costs to be borne by defendent). | |

116

## IDAHO

<u>1984 Legislation:</u>
   Nothing passed.

Per Se:   .10 per se, .08 presumptive.
Drinking Age:   19 yrs.
Dram Shop Law:   none.
Open Container Prohibition:   For wine only.

Refusals to Submit:
   120 days admin. lic. revoc.

Driving under Revoc. License:
   1st Offense:   Max $500, mand. 2 day-6 mos. jail, additional 6 mos. lic. revoc., work-restricted
                  lic. avail.
   2nd Offense w/in 5 yrs.:   Max $1000, mand. 20 day-1 yr. jail, addditional 1 yr. hard lic. revoc.
   3rd Offense w/in 5 yrs.:   Felony, max $3000, mand. 30 days-3 yrs. jail, additional 3 yrs. hard lic.
   revoc.

Youth Offender Legislation:
   1 yr. lic. revoc. or until 18th birthday, whichever is longer, for DUI offense.
   60 day lic. revoc. for underage (19 yrs.) possession violation (does not have to be DUI).

| | Penalties | Jail/CommSvc | LicRevoc/Rehab/Therapy | Other |
|---|---|---|---|---|
| 1st Offense | Misdemeanor, max $1000. | Max. 6 mos. jail. | 180 days lic. revoc., work-restricted lic. avail. | Be advised by Court, in writing, penalties for subsequent offenses. |
| 2nd Offense w/in 5 yrs. | Misdemeanor, Max $2000. | Mand. 10 days-1 yr. jail. | Mand. 6 mos.-1 yr. lic. revoc., work-restricted lic. avail. after 30 days. | Be advised by Court, in writing, penalties for subsequent offenses. |
| 3rd Offense w/in 5 yrs. | Felony, max. $5000. | Mand. 30 days-5 yrs. jail. | Mand. 1-5 yrs. lic. revoc. | |
| Aggravated DUI (injury occured) | Can be charged under Felony (3rd offense) statute. | | | Also includes restitution. |
| Vehicular homicide w/ gross negligence | $2000-7000. | and/or 2-7 yrs. jail. | Mand. hard lic. revoc. | |

## ILLINOIS

<u>1984 Legislation:</u>
    <u>SB1484</u> - If DUI and operating school bus, Class 4 felony.

Per Se: .10
Drinking Age: 21 yrs.
Dram Shop Law: Yes, liability limited to $20,000
Open Container Prohibition: Yes, driver assessed points for violation.

Refusals to Submit:
    Not technically administrative. If hearing is requested, it is judicial, not administrative hearing. Supposed to be separate issue, but often plea bargained as part of criminal proceedings.
    1st refusal: 6 mos. lic. revoc. Restricted lic. avail., but very difficult to get.
    2nd refusal: 12 mos. lic. revoc. Restricted lic. avail., but very difficult to get.

Driving under DUI Revoc. License:
    Class A misdemeanor. Mand. 7 days jail or 30 days comm. svc. Double orig. liv. revoc. period.

|  | Penalties | Jail/CommSvc | LicRevoc/Rehab/Therapy | Other |
|---|---|---|---|---|
| 1st Offense | Class A misdemeanor, max. $1000 | Max. 1 yr. jail | Mand. 1 yr. lic. revoc. Restricted lic. avail, but <u>very</u> difficult to get. | <u>OR</u> court supervision, max $1000, max. 2 yrs. lic. revoc, comm. svc. |
| 2nd Offense w/in 5 yrs. | Class A misdemeanor | Mand. 48 hrs. jail or 10 days comm. svc. | Mand. 1 yr. lic. revoc., hardship lic. avail, but <u>very</u> difficult to get. Rehab. | |

## INDIANA

<u>1984 Legislation:</u>
    <u>SB93</u> - Creates habitual offender statute - 3 or more DWIs or 2 or more DWIs where death occured. 10 yr. admin. lic. revoc.

    <u>SB94</u> - If refuse BAC test, admin. lic. revoc. period (90 days-2 yrs.) is in addition to criminal disposition. If .10, admin. lic. revoc. period is credited toward criminal lic. revoc. sentence. Changes mandatory 2 days jail for 2nd offenders to mandatory 48 hrs.

Per Se: .10
Drinking Age: 21 yrs.
Dram Shop Law: No dram shop statute, but prohibition against furnishing alcohol to intoxicated person. Appears to be case law to back up the liability of a seller for injuries caused by intoxicated person.
Open Container Prohibition: none.
Section 408 Grant: Received $1,206,503 Alcohol/Traffic Safety Grant (Basic and Supplemental).

Refusals to Submit:
    1 yr. admin. lic. revoc., admissible as evidence.

.10 Administrative Revocation:
    180 days, but credited against criminal disposition.

**118**

Driving under Revoc. License:
Class D felony, max. $10,000, mand. 5 days-4 yrs. jail.  3 yrs.-permanent lic. revoc.

| | Penalties | Jail/CommSvc | LicRevoc/Rehab/Therapy | Other |
|---|---|---|---|---|
| 1st Offense DWI (not necessarily .10) | Class A misdemeanor, max. $5000 | Max. 1 yr. jail. | 90 day lic. revoc. or 180 day probation with 30 day hard and 60 day restricted lic. revoc. | |
| 1st Offense .10 | Class C misdemeanor, max $500 | Max. 60 days jail. | 90 day lic. revoc. or 180 day probation and 30 day hard and 60 day restricted lic. revoc. | |
| 2nd Offense w/in 5 yrs., or if bodily injury | Class D felony, max. $10,000. | Mand. 5 days jail (48 hrs. consecutive) or 10 days comm. svc.-4 yrs. jail. | 1-2 yrs. lic. revoc. | |
| If death occurs | Class C felony, max. $10,000. | 5-8 yrs. jail. | 1-2 yrs. lic. revoc. | |

Miscellaneous:
Prosecutor must notify victims of trial date at least 10 days prior.


# IOWA

### 1984 Legislation:
HF2486 - Major revision of penalties.

HF2472 - Open container prohibition, parents to be notified of underage drinking violations.

HF2235 - relating to driving under revoc. lic.

Per Se:  .13, .10 for administrative revocation.
Drinking Age:  19 yrs.
Dram Shop Law: Yes, §123.92
Open Container Prohibition:  new (see HF2472).

Refusals to Submit (administratively imposed):
1st refusal:  240 days. lic. revoc. (was 180 days).
2nd refusal:  540 days lic. revoc. (was 1 yr.), work-restricted lic. avail. after 365 days.

.10 Admin. Revoc. Penalties (regardless of criminal disposition):
1st Offense:  180 days lic. revoc. (was 120 days), work-restricted lic. avail.
2nd Offense:  1 yr. lic. revoc. (was 240 days), work-restricted lic. avail.

119

| | Penalties | Jail/CommSvc | LicRevoc/Rehab/Therapy | Other |
|---|---|---|---|---|
| 1st Offense | Serious Misdemeanor, $500-1000, <u>OR</u> 50-200 hrs. comm. svc. | Mand. 48 hrs. jail. | 30-90 days. lic. revoc. | |
| 2nd Offense w/in 6 yrs. | Aggravated misdemeanor, min. $750. | Mand. 7 days jail. | Lic. revoc. until rehab., restricted lic. avail. if plead guilty. | Substance abuse evaluation in-patient time can be credited against sentence. |
| 3rd Offense w/in 6 yrs. | Class D felony, min. $750. | | Min. 2-6 yr. lic. revoc. | Substance abuse evaluation in-patient time can be credited against sentence. |
| If serious injury occured | Class D felony, min. $750. | | Additional 1 yr. lic. revoc., work-restricted lic. avail. | |
| If death occured | Class D felony, min. $750. | | Addition 6 yrs. lic. revoc. | Restitution. |

Miscellaneous:
   <u>$100 assessment</u> (civil penalty) for all lic. revoc.


# KENTUCKY

<u>1984 Legislation:</u>
   <u>SB20</u> - Major revision of DWI statute, see below.

Per Se:  No per se; .10 presumptive; if .15 BAC, person to be detained at least 4 hrs.
Drinking Age:  21 yrs.
Dram Shop Law:  No specific statute, except it is illegal to sell to intoxicated person.  May be some
                weak case law supporting liability of vendor.
Open Container Prohibition:  None.
PBTs:  Allowed, refusal not admissible.

Refusals to Submit:
   6 mos. admin. lic. revoc.  Work-restricted lic. avail. for 1st refusals if enroll in rehab.

Driving under Revoc. License:
   1st Offense:  Class B misdemeanor, 2x orig. lic. revoc. period.
   2nd Offense:  Class A misdemeanor, 2x orig. lic. revoc. period.

Youth Offender Legislation:
    If convicted, lic. to be revoc. until 18th birthday or according to sentence, whichever is longer period.

| | Penalties | Jail/CommSvc | LicRevoc/Rehab/Therapy | Other |
|---|---|---|---|---|
| 1st Offense | $200-500 | &/OR 48 hrs.-30 days jail (can be served on weekends) OR 2-30 days comm. svc. if no injury. | 6 mos. lic. revoc. OR rehab. and 30 day lic. revoc. | Jail mand. if injury occured. |
| 2nd Offense | Mand. $350-500. | Mand. 7 days-6 mos. jail (can be served on weekends) 10 days-6 mos. comm. svc. | Mand. 12 mos. lic. revoc. Max. 1 yr. rehab. | |
| 3rd Offense | Mand. $500-1000. | Mand. 30 days-12 mos. jail. 10 days-12 mos. comm. svc. | Mand. 24 mos. lic. revoc. Mand. 1 yr. rehab. | |

Miscellaneous:
    Additional $150 assessed on all convictions, used to fund DWI law.

## LOUISIANA

1984 Legislation:
    HB1051 (Act 511) - Allows exemplary damages (in addition to general and special damages) to be awarded when DWI caused injuries occur.

    SB612 (Act 409) - Non-substantive technical changes relating to admin. lic. revoc. procedures.

Per Se: .10
Drinking Age: 18 yrs.
Dram Shop Law: No statute, except illegal to sell to intoxicated person.
Open Container Prohibition: None.
Sec. 408 Grant: Received $527,956 (Basic only. Has not yet submitted Supplemental Grant information. Will receive additional $351,971 when that is done.)

Refusals to Submit:
    1st refusal: 90 days hard admin. lic. revoc., 90 days restricted lic.
    2nd refusal: 545 days hard admin. lic. revoc.

Administrative Lic. Revoc. for .10:
    1st Offense: 90 days admin. lic. revoc.
    2nd Offense: 365 days hard admin. lic. revoc.

DWI and Driving under Revoc. License:
    $300-500, mand. 7 days-6 mos. jail.

|  | Penalties* | Jail/CommSvc | LicRevoc/Rehab/Therapy | Other |
|---|---|---|---|---|
| 1st Offense | $125-500, | 10 days-6 mos. jail, | 60 days lic. revoc., restricted lic. avail. |  |
| OR if probation |  | 2 days jail or 32 hrs. comm. svc., | Rehab., including assessment. |  |
| 2nd Offense | $300-500, | 30 days-6 mos. jail, | 1 yr. hard lic. revoc. |  |
| OR if probation |  | 15 days jail or 30 days comm. svc., | Rehab., including assessment. |  |
| 3rd Offense | Max. $1000, | 6 mos.-5 yrs. jail, | 1 yr. hard lic. revoc., rehab. including assessment. |  |
| 4th Offense |  | 10-30 yrs. hard labor imprisonment. | 1 yr. hard lic. revoc. |  |
| Vehicular Homicide while DWI | $2000-5000, | 2-5 yrs. jail. |  |  |
| Vehicular Injury while DWI | Max. $500, | and/or 6 mos. jail. |  |  |

\* All penalties are min. mand. unless stated.

Miscellaneous:
   Owner of vehicle notified if car involved in DWI offense.

## MAINE

**1984 Legislation:**
   Nothing passed.

**Per Se:** .10
**Drinking Age:** 20 yrs.
**Dram Shop Law:** Citing responsibilities by seller/giver when giving alcohol to intoxicated person.
**Open Container Prohibition:** None, except if under 20 yrs. old cannot transport liquor at all unless at request of employer or parent.
**Section 408 Grant:** Received $262,000 Alcohol/Traffic Safety Grant (Basic and Supplemental).

**Refusals to Submit** (administratively imposed and admissible as evidence):
   1st refusal: 180 day lic. revoc., work-restricted lic. avail.
   2nd refusal w/in 6 yrs: 1 yr. lic. revoc., work-restricted lic. avail.

**Driving under Revoc. License:**
   Class D crime, maximum $2500.

**Youth Offender Legislation:**
   Provisional lic. until driver is 20 yrs. old. 1 yr. lic. revoc. for DWI, or if .02 BAC or if refusal to submit. Work-restricted lic. avail. after 6 mos. if rehab. is completed.

|  | Penalties | Jail/CommSvc | LicRevoc/Rehab/Therapy | Other |
|---|---|---|---|---|
| 1st Offense traffic infraction | Mand. min. $250-500 |  | Mand. min. 45-135 days lic. revoc. |  |

| | | | | |
|---|---|---|---|---|
| 1st Offense criminal violation if BAC above .20, driving 30 mph over limit, Or if eluded police; Or if 2nd Offense w/in 6 yrs. | Class D crime, mand. min. $350 | Mand. min. 48 hrs. jail | Mand. 90-275 days lic. revoc., or 2/3 of revoc. period and rehab. | |
| 2nd Offense criminal violation | Same as above, | | EXCEPT mand. 1 yr. lic. revoc., or 2/3 of revoc. period and rehab. | |
| 3rd Offense criminal violation | Habitual offender, $5000 | Mand. 60 days jail | Indefinite lic. revoc. | |
| If homicide occurs | | | 5 yrs. permanent lic. revoc. | |

## MARYLAND

### 1984 Legislation:

HB636 - BAC tests are admissible without presence of person who performed test.

HB749 - Relating to time frame for which defendent can notify BAC technician to be present at trial.

HB900 - State's Attorney to be notified if juvenile fails to comply with rehab. or work program.

SB367 - Clarifies that if BAC test required by police, certain equipment standards must be met.

Per Se: No per se; .13 prima facie for DWI, .08 prima facie for DWUI.
Drinking Age: 21 yrs.
Dram Shop Law: Although statute prohibiting sales to intoxicated people exists, court has ruled that does not expand to include dram shop law.
Open Container Prohibition: None for moving m.v. Applies only to parked vehicles in parking lots.
PBTs: Allowed, but refusal to submit is not violation.

Refusals to Submit (administratively imposed):
    1st refusal: Mand. 60 days-6 mos. lic. revoc. Work-restricted lic. avail.
    2nd refusal: Mand. 120 days-1 yr. lic. revoc. Work-restricted lic. avail.

Driving under Revoc. License (12 pts.):
    1st Offense: Max. $1000, 1 yr. jail.; 120 day vehicle registration suspension.
    2nd Offense: Same as above, except 2 yrs. jail.

| DWI .13 BAC | Penalties | Jail/CommSvc | LicRevoc/Rehab/Therapy | Other |
|---|---|---|---|---|
| 1st Offense | Max. $1000, | 1 yr. jail. | 6 mos. lic. revoc., if probation then rehab. | |
| 2nd Offense w/in 3 yrs. | Max. $1000, | 2 yrs. jail. | 1 yr. lic. revoc., if probation then rehab. | |
| 3rd Offense w/in 3 yrs. | Max. $1000, | 2 yrs. jail. | 18 mos. lic. revoc., if probation then rehab. | |
| **DWUI .08 BAC** | | | | |
| 1st Offense | Max. $500, | Max. 1 yr. jail. | 60 day lic. revoc., if probation then rehab. | |

| | | | | |
|---|---|---|---|---|
| 2nd Offense w/in 3 yrs. | Max. $500, | Max. 1 yr. jail. | Max. 129 days lic. revoc., if probation then rehab. | |
| 3rd Offense w/in 3 yrs. | Max. $500, | Max. 1 yr. jail. | Max. 6 mos. lic. revoc. If probation then 6 mos. lic. revoc. | |

## MASSACHUSETTS

1984 Legislation:

Approximately 11 bills pending, including:

HB5952 - to raise legal drinking age to 21 yrs.  Has passed House, and in Senate Ways & Means Committee as of 8/15/84.

S2152 - Establishes .10 per se offense.

S2106 - Establishes .10 per se offense and increases/clarifies ceretain other penalties for repeat offenders.

H1357 - Info. on conviction shall also be sent to establishment that allegedly served violator.

H2110 - Deletes ability to serve sentence on weekends, evenings and holidays.

H2488 - Additional $100 penalty for DWI to fund Victim Compensation Fund.

H2688 - Mandates driver ed. courses to include DWI info.

H5589 - Repeals provision requiring DWI violator to give name and location of establishment where alcohol was obtained.

Per Se: None.

Drinking Age:  21 yrs.

Dram Shop Law:  Illegal to sell to intoxicated person.  Case law supports 3rd party (dram shop) liability (138 §69).

Open Container Prohibition:  $100-500 (adopted 1982).

Refusals to Submit:

90 days admin. lic. revoc.  If hearing requested, revoc. not stayed.

Driving under DWI Revoc. License:

$200-500, mand. 7 days-2 yrs. jail.

| | Penalties | Jail/CommSvc | LicRevoc/Rehab/Therapy | Other |
|---|---|---|---|---|
| 1st Offense | $100-1000, | Max. 2 days jail, 36 hrs. comm. svc. | Mand. 1 yr. lic. revoc. | |
| | OR 2 yrs. probation*, $100-1000, | Max. 2 days jail, 36 hrs. comm. svc., | Mand. 30 days lic. revoc., 14 day residential treatment program, | Additional $200 assessment to support program. |
| 2nd Offense w/in 6 yrs.s | $300-1000, | Mand. 7 days--2 yrs. jail, 36 hrs. comm. svc. | Mand. 1 yr. hard lic. revoc., 1 yr. restricted lic. | |
| | OR 2 yrs. probation* if never rec'd before, $300-1000, | Mand. 7 days-2 yrs. jail, 36 hrs. comm. svc. | Mand. 1 yr.. hard lic. revoc., 2 yrs. restricted lic., 14 day residential treatment program, | Additional $200 assessment. |

| | | | | |
|---|---|---|---|---|
| 3rd Offense w/in 6 yrs. | $500-1000, | Mand. 60 days-2 yrs. jail, 36 hrs. comm. svc., | Mand. 3 yrs. hard lic. revoc., 2 yrs. restricted lic. | |
| Homicide by M.V. - 1st Offense | Max. $5000, | 1-10 yrs. jail, | 10 yrs. lic. revoc. | |
| Homicide by M.V. - 2nd Offense | Max. $5000, | 1-10 yrs. jail, | Permanent lic. revoc. | |

\* No probation available if death/serious injury occured.

Miscellaneous:
In all convictions, court shall obtain name and address of establishment where defendent was served alcohol prior to the violation.


## MICHIGAN

1984 Legislation:
All still pending in Committee, on recess until September 11, 1984.
HB4397 - Assesses 1 pt. penalty for open container violation. Current law has 2 pt. penalty.

HB4443 - Assesses 3 pt. penalty for violations of open container law.

HB4472 - Adds mand. 48 hrs. jail or 80 days comm. svc. for 2nd offenders. Changes 1st refusals from fine or jail to fine and jail. Additional changes relating to minor drivers.

HB4681 - Technical change, court not required to authorize assessment, but if it does, it can designate person or agency to do assessment.

HB4717 - Allows Court probation department to do assessment.

HB5675 - Youth Offender Legislation; cannot drive with any BAC in system.

Per Se: .10
Drinking Age: 21 yrs.
Dram Shop Law: Yes, §18.993
Open Container Prohibition: Yes.

Refusals to Submit:
1st refusal: 6 mos. admin. lic. revoc.
2nd refusal: 1 yr. admin. lic. revoc.

Driving under Revoc. License:
1st Offense: Max. $100, or 3-90 days jail, registration plates confiscated. Double original lic. revoc.
2nd Offense: Max $500, 5 days-1 yr. jail, other provisions same as above.

| | Penalties | Jail/CommSvc | LicRevoc/Rehab/Therapy | Other |
|---|---|---|---|---|
| 1st Offense DWI .10 | Misdemeanor, $100-500, | Max. 90 days jail. Max. 12 days comm. svc. | 6 mos.-2 yrs. lic. revoc., restricted lic. avail. | Prosecution costs, pre-sentence assessment/ rehab. |
| 2nd Offense w/in 7 yrs. | Max. $1000 | And/or max. 1 yr. jail. Max. 12 days comm. svc. | Mand. lic revoc. | Pre-sentence assessment/ rehab. |
| 3rd Offense w/in 10 yrs. | Felony, | Max. 12 days comm. svc. | Mand. lic. revoc. | Pre-sentencce assessment/ rehab. |
| 1st Offense Operating While Impaired (.07-.09 BAC) | $300, | Max. 90 days jail. Max. 12 days comm. svc. | 90 days-1 yr. lic. revoc. | Pre-sentencce assessment/ rehab. |

| 2nd Offense w/in 7 yrs. of either OWI or .10 | Max. $1000, | Max. 1 yr. jail. Max. 12 days comm. svc. | Mand. 6-18 mos. lic. revoc., including 60 day hard. | |
|---|---|---|---|---|

Miscellaneous:
Statute provides for annual drunk driving audit to be prepared each year showing number of alcohol-related m.v. accidents, injuries, deaths, arrests made, lic. suspensions, convictions and penalties assessed.

## MINNESOTA

### 1984 Legislation:
SF473 (Ch. 306) - Related to police arrest powers. Can arrest outside jurisdiction if police believe probable cause exists and driver eludes officer. Allows refusal to be admissible as evidence with no restrictions.

SF1642 (Ch.. 430) - Allows use of infrared breath test equipment.

SF1336 (Ch. 622) - Allows defense to per se law that defendent consumed the alcohol after the time of actual driving but before BAC test was given. This defense, if used, must be given to prosecution prior to pre-trial hearing. Youth Offender Legislation: lic. revoc. for 6 mos. or until 18th birthday (whichever is longer) for DWI violation; restricted lic. avail only if needed for school or rehab; 30 days lic. revoc. for minors purchasing alcohol if drivers lic. used in attempt. Strengthens refusal penalties; was 6 mos, now it is 1 yr. Expands DWI jurisdiction to include public parking lots.

Per Se: .10, .07 recorded on lic., upon 2nd stop of .07, assessment may be required.
Drinking Age: 19 yrs.
Dram Shop Law: Statute in effect, 1982 amendment deleted maximum dollar amount recoverable (§340.95).
Open Container Prohibition: Yes.
PBTs: Allowed, not admissible as evidence.

Refusals to Submit:
Admissible as evidence (new). 1 yr. admin. lic. revoc. (new). Revoc. not stayed even if hearing is requested.

.10 BAC:
90 days admin. lic. revoc. Revoc. not stayed even if hearing is requested.

Driving under Revoc. License:
Misdemeanor, max. $500, 30 days jail.

DWI and Under Revoc. Liicense:
Gross Misdemeanor, max. $1000, 90 days jail.

Youth Offender Legislation:
If DWI, 6 mos. admin. lic. revoc., or until age 18 yrs, whichever is longer. Also 30 days lic. revoc. for minors purchasing alcohol using drivers lic.

| | Penalties | Jail/CommSvc | LicRevoc/Rehab/Therapy | Other |
|---|---|---|---|---|
| 1st Offense | Max. $500, | 90 days jail, | Mand. 30 days lic. revoc.* | |
| 2nd Offense w/in 5 yrs. | Gross misdemeanor, max. $1000, | Max. 1 yr. jail, | Mand. 90 days lic. revoc., and rehab.* | |
| 3rd Offense w/in 5 yrs. | Gross misdemeanor, max. $1000, | Max. 1 yr. jail, | Mand. 1 yr. lic. revoc., and rehab.* | |
| 4th Offense w/in 5 yrs. | Gross misdemeanor, max. $1000, | Max. 1 yr. jail, | Mand. 2 yrs. lic. revoc., and rehab.* | |
| If personal injury | | | Additional 90 days lic. revoc. | |
| DWI death & gross negligence (driver does not stop) | Felony, $5000, | 5 yrs. jail. | | |
| DWI injury & gross negligence (driver does not stop) | Felony, $3000, | 3 yrs. jail. | | |

* Restricted lic. avail. immediately except if manslaughter, gross negligence or felony.

# MISSISSIPPI

<u>1984 Legislation:</u>
Nothing passed.

Per Se:  .10
Drinking Age:  18 yrs. for beer with less than 4% alcohol and light wine, 21 yrs. for everything else.
Dram Shop Law:  No specific statute, but is illegal to sell/furnish alcohol to intoxicated person.
Open Container Prohibition:  none.
Section 408 Grant:  Received $646,055 Alcohol/Traffic Safety Grant (Basic and Supplemental).
PBTs:  Allowed.

Refusals to Submit (administratively imposed):
   $500-1000, and/or 1 yr., jail.  90 day lic. revoc, 45 days hard suspension.

Driving under Revoc. License:
   Misdemeanor, $200-500, 48 hrs.-6 mos. jail.  Additional 6 mos. lic. revoc.

| | Penalties | Jail/CommSvc | LicRevoc/Rehab/Therapy | Other |
|---|---|---|---|---|
| 1st Offense | $200-5000, | And/or 24 hrs. jail. | 1 yr. lic. revoc. or 90 days and ASAP.  Work-restricted lic. avail after 45 days. | |
| 2nd Offense w/in 5 yrs. | $400-1000. | 48 hrs.-1 yr. jail or comm. svc. | 2 yr. lic revoc. or 1 yr. lic. revoc. and rehab. | |
| 3rd Offense w/in 5 yrs. | $500-1000, | 30 days-1 yr. jail. | 3 yr. lic. revoc. or 1 yr. and rehab. | |
| If death occurs | Felony, max. 5 yrs. jail. | | | |

Miscellaneous:
   If .10 BAC: Lic. pulled and 30 day temp. given pending disposition of criminal charges.  (Not strictly administrative revoc. because of tie-in to crim. charges.)
   No plea bargaining if .10+ BAC.

# MISSOURI

<u>1984 Legislation:</u>
   SB608/681 - Prohibits imposition of administrative lic. revoc. if arrest was based upon roadblock/checkpoint stop in which there was no probable cause to stop.

   HB1226 - Expands Crime Victims Compensation Fund to include DWI victims.

Per Se:  .10 per se, administrative lic. revoc. at .13.
Drinking Age:  21 yrs.
Dram Shop Law:  No specific law, although some case law to back up joint negligence of tavern owner and intoxicated person (Carver vs. Schafer (App. 1983) 647 SW.2d 570).
Open Container Prohibition:  none

Refusals to Submit (administratively imposed):
   1 yr. lic revocation.

Administrative License Revocation for .13 BAC:
   Cannot be imposed if arrest occured at roadblock/checkpoint (new, see SB60/681).  May be credited against later criminal revocation.
   1st Offense: 30 day hard lic. revoc., 60 day restricted lic. revoc., rehab.
   2nd Offense: 1 yr. hard lic. revoc. and rehab.

Driving under Revoc. License:
   Class A misdemeanor, $100, mandatory 48 hrs.-1 yr. jail or 10 days (40 hrs.) comm. svc.

127

| | Penalties | Jail/CommSvc | LicRevoc/Rehab/Therapy | Other |
|---|---|---|---|---|
| 1st Offense DWI (not necessarily .10) | Class B misdemeanor, $500, | Max. 6 mos. jail. | 30 days lic. revoc. | All mandatory unless min. 2 yr. probation is given. |
| 1st Offense w/.10 BAC | Class C misdemeanor, $300, | Max. 15 days jail. | No lic. revoc. stipulated. | |
| 2nd Offense w/in 5 yrs. | Prior offender, Class A misdemeanor, $1000. | Mand. 48 hrs.-1 yr. jail or 10 days comm. svc. (40 hrs.) | Mand. 1 yr. lic. revoc. | |
| 3rd Offense w/in 5 yrs. | Persistent offender, Class D felony, $5000, | 1-5 yrs. jail, min. mand. 1/3 of jail term must be served. | Mand. 1 yr. lic. revoc. | |

## MONTANA

1984 Legislation:
   None; did not meet.

Per Se:  .10
Drinking Age:  19 yrs.
Dram Shop Law:  No law, except illegal to sell to intoxicated person.
Open Container Prohibition:  Yes.
Section 408 Grant:  Received $363,265 Alcohol/Traffic Safety Grant (Basic and Supplemental).

Refusals to Submit (administratively imposed, refusal admissible as evidence):
   1st refusal:  90 days hard lic. revoc.
   2nd refusal:  1 yr. hard lic. revoc.

Driving under Revoc. License:
   Misdemeanor, max. $500, 2 days-6 mos. jail.  2x/initial revoc. period.

| DWI (below .10) | Penalties | Jail/CommSvc | LicRevoc/Rehab/Therapy | Other |
|---|---|---|---|---|
| 1st Offense | $100-500 | Mand. 24 hrs.-60 days jail, unless judge feels imposition poses risk to defendents physical/mental well-being. | Mand. 6 mos. lic. revoc. Rehab. | |
| 2nd Offense w/in 5 yrs | $300-500 | Mand. 4 days (at least 48 hrs. consecutive)-6 mos. jail. | Mand. 1 yr. lic. revoc. Rehab. | |

| | | | | |
|---|---|---|---|---|
| 3rd Offense w/in 5 yrs | $500-1000 | Mand 10 days (at least 48 hrs. consecutive)-1 yr. jail. | Mand. 1 yr. lic. revoc. Rehab. | |
| **.10** | | | | |
| 1st Offense | $100-500 | Max. 10 days jail. | Mand. 6 mos. lic. revoc. Rehab. | |
| 2nd Offense w/in 5 yrs. | $300-500 | 48 hrs.-30 days jail | Mand. 1 yr. lic. revoc. Rehab. | |
| 3rd Offense w/in 5 yrs. | $500-1000 | 48 hrs.-6 mos. jail. | Mand. 1 yr. lic. revoc. Rehab. | |

## NEBRASKA

**1984 Legislation:**
  LB56 - Raises drinking age from 20 to 21 yrs.

Per Se: .10
Drinking Age: 21 yrs.
Dram Shop Law: No statute; illegal to sell to intoxicated person, but no 3rd party (dram shop) liability
   created.
Open Container Prohibition: None.

Refusals to Submit to PBT or .10 BAC:
  1st Offense: Class W misdemeanor, 6 mos. hard admin. lic. revoc., or, if probation, 60 days hard.
     lic. revoc.
  2nd Offense: Class W misdemeanor, 1 yr. hard admin. lic. revoc., or, if probation, 6 mos. hard.
     lic. revoc., 48 hrs. jail.
  3rd Offense: Permanent lic. revoc., or, if probation, 1 yr. hard licc. revoc., 7 days jail.

Refusal to submit:               Operating under Revoc. License:
  1 yr. hard admin. lic. revoc.       Class IV felony

| | Penalties | Jail/CommSvc | LicRevoc/Rehab/Therapy | Other |
|---|---|---|---|---|
| 1st Offense | Class W misdemeanor, $200, | Mand. 7 days jail, | Mand. 6 mos. hard lic.. revoc. | OR probation, mand. 60 days hard lic. revoc. |
| 2nd Offense | Class W misdemeanor, $500, | Mand. 30 days jail, | Mand. 6 mos. hard lic. revoc. | OR probation, mand. 48 hrs. jail, mand. 6 mos. hard lic. revoc. |
| 3rd Offense | Class W misdemeanor, $500, | Mand. 6 mos. jail, | Mand. permanent lic. revoc. | OR probation, mand. 7 days jail, mand. 1 yr. hard lic. revoc. |

## NEVADA

<u>1984 Legislation:</u>
None, did not meet.

Per Se: .10
Drinking Age: 21 yrs.
Dram Shop Law: None.
Open Container Prohibition: Partial; illegal to drink while driving.
Section 408 Grant: Received $273,488 Alcohol/Traffic Safety Grant (Basic and Supplemental).
PBTs: Allowed, not admissible as evidence.

Refusals to Submit:
    1st refusal: 1 yr. lic. revoc.
    2nd refusal: 3 yrs. lic. revoc.

Driving under Revoc. License:
    Mand. $500-1000, mand 30 days-6 mos. jail does not have to be served consecutively. Double original lic. revoc.

Refusal to submit to PBT or if .10 BAC:
    90 days admin. lic. revoc.

| | Penalties* | Jail/CommSvc | LicRevoc/Rehab/Therapy | Other |
|---|---|---|---|---|
| 1st Offense w/in 7 yrs. | Misdemeanor, $200-1000, | 2 days-6 mos. jail or 48 hrs. comm. svc. (dressed in manner to identify as violator of law), | 90 days lic. revoc, 45 days hard., | Education. OR probation, max. $200, 1 day jail or 24 hrs. comm. svc., 45 day lic revoc. Prosecutor has right to request hearing on probation. |
| 2nd Offense w/in 7 yrs. | Misdemeanor, $500-1000, | 10 days-6 mos. jail (at least 48 hrs. consecutive), | 1 yr. hard lic. revoc. | OR probation, max. $500, 5 days jail (at least 48 hrs. consecutive), rehab., 6 mos. lic revoc. Prosecutor has right to request hearing on probation. |
| 3rd Offense w/in 7 yrs., or if death/injury occured | $2000-5000, | 1-6 yrs. jail (segregated from violent offenders), | 3 yrs. hard lic. revoc. | |

* all penalties minimum mandatory.

Miscellaneous:
    <u>Can require more than 1 BAC test.</u> Failure to submit to either or both constitute failure.

## NEW HAMPSHIRE

<u>1984 Legislation:</u>
None; did not meet.

Per Se: .10
Drinking Age: 20 yrs.
Dram Shop Law: Illegal to serve intoxicated person, act of negligence, but no specific dram shop statute.
Open Container Prohibition: Applies only if under 20 yrs. old, traveling without parent/legal guardian.
Sec. 408 Grant: Received $262,000 Alcohol/Traffic Safety Grant (Basic and Supplemental).

Refusals to Submit (administratively imposed for refusals, but not .10; admissable as evidence):
   1st refusal: 90 days lic. revoc.
   2nd refusal: 1 yr. lic. revoc.
   This revoc. period to run consecutively with any other periods of lic. revoc.

Driving under Revoc. License:
   $100, mandatory 7 days jail (to be served consecutively within 6 months). 1 yr. lic. revoc.

| | Penalties | Jail/CommSvc | LicRevoc/Rehab/Therapy | Other |
|---|---|---|---|---|
| 1st Offense | Max. $1000. | | Min. Mand. 90 days-2 yrs. lic. revoc. | |
| 2nd Offense w/in 7 yrs. | Misdemeanor, max. $1000, | Mand. 7 days jail (served consecutively w/in 6 mos.) | Mand. 3 yrs. lic. revoc. | Liable for double damages in civil suit. |
| 3rd Offense | | | Mand. 3 yrs.-permanent lic. revoc. | |
| Aggravated DWI - <br> 1) If impaired or .10 BAC and driving 30 mph above posted limit and either - bodily injury occured, or - tried to elude police <br><br> 2) If BAC above .20 | misdemeanor, $350-1000. | | 1 yr. lic. revoc. | |

Miscellaneous:
   Plea bargaining from 2nd offense to 1st offense and, to non-alcohol offenses if BAC is .10+, is restricted.
   Limits continuation of cases for more than 35 days.
   BAC tests taken from all deceased drivers and pedestrians can be used for statistical eveluations or as evidence in trial actions.

## NEW JERSEY

1984 Legislation:
   AB802 (CH.1) - Surcharge on insurance for DWI convictions and/or increase in points.

   AB828 (Ch.4) - Additional $100 assessment for Drunk Driving Enforcement Fund.

   Pending legislation, on recess subject to call of chair:
   AB223 - DMV to apply penalties of state in which violation occured, if penalties are weaker than N.J.

   AB311 - Alcohol servers and retailers to post DWI laws on their premises.

   AB849 - N.J. Commission to Deter Criminal Activity (already in existence) to advertise DWI penalties.

   SB1107 - Allows DMV greater latitude in revoking licences without a hearing, e.g. if .10 BAC, refused BAC test, 3rd moving violation w/in 3 yrs, death or injury resulted.

   SB1204 - Relating to AB802(ch.1). Allows 1 yr. grace period (to 1/1/84) before violations are to be considered for this insurance surcharge.

   SB1296 - Strengthens penalties for driving under revoked license, including mand. sentences.

   SB1697 - Strengthens penalties for 3rd and subsequent offenders.

Per Se:  .10
Drinking Age:  21 yrs.
Dram Shop Law:  Extends liability of seller to both third parties and intoxicated persons themselves.
33:1-39 Note 10.  Recent N.J. case also expands liability to include private party
host/hostess who serves intoxicated person.
Open Container Prohibition:  $200-250, 10 days comm. svc.
Section 408 Grant:  Received $796,474 Alcohol/Traffic Safety Grant (Basic only.  In order do qualify for
Supplemental Incentive Grant, state must revoke lic. within 45 days of arrest, or
within 90 days of arrest and submit plan to reduce it to 45 days.)

Refusals to Submit:
1st refusal:  $250-500, mand. 6 mos. admin. lic. revoc.
2nd refusal:  $250-500, mand 2 yrs. admin. lic. revoc.

Driving under DUI Revoc. License:
$1000, mand. 30 days jail (45 days if injury occured).

|  | Penalties | Jail/CommSvc | LicRevoc/Rehab/Therapy | Other |
|---|---|---|---|---|
| 1st Offense | $250-400, | 30 days jail, | 6 mos.-1 yr. lic. revoc. | |
| 2nd Offense w/in 10 yrs. | $500-1000, | Mand. 90 days jail or 30 days comm. svc. | Mand. 2 yrs. lic. revoc., mand. 30 days rehab. | |
| 3rd Offense w/in 10 yrs. | Mand. $1000, | Mand. 180 days jail or 90 days jail/ 90 days comm. svc. | Mand. 10 yr. lic. revoc. | |
| Death by m.v. due to DUI | 4th degree, | Additional mand. 120 days jail. | | |

# NEW MEXICO

1984 Legislation:
HB67 (ch. 72) - Clarifies .10 per se law; adds administrative lic. revoc for .10.  Prohibits
work-restricted lic. for refusals and 2nd offenders.  Administrative revocations and subsequent
criminal revocation penalties to total maximum 1 yr.  Prohibits refusals if great bodily injury
occured.  Youth offender legislation stipulates admin. lic. revoc. if less than 18 yrs old and BAC
is .05.

HB75 (ch. 73) - Technical amendment appropriates funds for administrative revocation.

Per Se:  .10
Drinking Age:  21 yrs.
Dram Shop Law:  none
Open Container Prohibition:  none
Section 408 Grant:  Received $389,777 Alcohol/Traffic Safety Grant (Basic and Supplemental)

Refusals to Submit (administratively imposed):
1 yr. lic. revoc.

Administrative License Revocation (.10 for over 18 yr. olds, .05 for under 18 yr. olds):
1st Offense:  90 days for 18 yr. olds and older.  6 mos. if under 18 yrs.
2nd Offense:  1 yr. if under 18 yrs. old.
All administrative lic. revoc. penalties to run concurrently with any criminal revocation penalties,
if so assessed (new, see HB67).

Driving Under Revoc. Lic.:
Misdemeanor, max. $500, 2 days-6 mos. jail, additional revocation.

| | Penalties | Jail/CommSvc | LicRevoc/Rehab/Therapy | Other |
|---|---|---|---|---|
| 1st Offense | $300-500, | 30-90 days jail, | Mand. 1 yr. lic. revoc, restricted lic. avail. | OR 90 days-3 yrs. probation. |
| 2nd Offense | $1000. | Mand. 48 hrs.-1 yr. jail, | Mand. 1 yr. hard lic. revoc. | OR 1-5 yrs. probation and mand. 48 hrs. jail instead of fine. |
| Homicide or great bodily injury by m.v. while DUI | 3rd degree felony, | | 1 yr. lic. revoc. | |

# NEW YORK

**1984 Legislation:**
S1254D - Deletes provision allowing completion of rehab. to satisfy one-half of fine or jail penalty.

Per Se:  .10
Drinking Age: 19 yrs. (21 yr. old bill failed in 1984)
Dram Shop Law:  Illegal to sell to intoxicated persons, case law supports 3rd party (dram shop) liability based upon this statute.
Open Container Prohibition: Yes

Refusals to Submit:
   Cannot refuse if accident occurs.
   1st refusal:  $100, mand. 6 mos. hard lic. revoc.
   1st refusal w/ prior conviction w/in 5 yrs.:  $250, mand. 1 yr. hard lic. revoc.
   2nd refusal w/in 5 yrs.:  $250, 1 yr. hard lic. revoc.

Driving under Revoc. License:
   Misdemeanor, $200-500, mand. 7-180 days (do not have to be served consecutively.)

Youth Offender Legislation:
   Lic. revoc. until age 21 for DWI (.10) conviction.
   $200, and/or 5 days jail for obtaining liquor for underage persons.  Also civilly liable for damages caused as a result of that procurement.

| DWAI (.06-.09 BAC) | Penalties | Jail/CommSvc | LicRevoc/Rehab/Therapy | Other |
|---|---|---|---|---|
| 1st Offense | Infraction, mand. $250, | Max. 15 days jail, | Mand. 90 days lic. revoc. | OR Drinking driver program, same penalties except restricted lic. avail. |
| 2nd Offense w/in 5 yrs. | Infraction, mand. $350-500, | Max. 30 days jail, | Mand. 6 mos. hard lic. revoc. | |
| 3rd Offense w/in 5 yrs. | Infraction, mand. $500-1500, | Max 90 days jail, | Mand. 6 mos. hard lic. revoc. | |
| DWI (.10) | | | | |
| 1st Offense | Misdemeanor, mand. $350-500, | Max. 1 yr. jail, | Mand. 6 mos. hard lic. revoc. | |

| 2nd Offense w/in 10 yrs. | Felony, mand. $500-5000, | Max. 4 yrs. jail, | Mand. 1 yr. lic. revoc. | |
|---|---|---|---|---|
| 2nd offense w/in 10 yrs., personal injury | Felony, mand. $500-5000, | Max. 4 yrs. jail, | Mand. permanent lic. revoc. | |
| Vehicular Assault | Class E felony, | Max. 4 yrs. jail, | Mand. 6 mos. lic. revoc. | |
| Vehicular Manslaughter | Class D felony, | Max. 7 yrs. jail, | Mand. 6 mos. lic. revoc. | |

Miscellaneous:

STOP-DWI (Special Traffic Options Program for DWI):
1981 legislation created funding mechanism for local drunk driving programs approved by state.
Provides return of fines from state to county, earmarked for DWI. Prohibits plea bargaining from DWI
to non-alcohol offense.

Insurance companies to provide clients with info. on current NY DWI-DWAI laws on an annual basis.


## NORTH CAROLINA

1984 Legislation:
HB1660 (ch. 1101) - Technical changes to last yr.'s bill.

Per Se: .10
Drinking Age: 19 yrs. for beer/table wine, 21 yrs. for everything else.
Dram Shop Law: Limited to minors, $500,000 limit of liability. Must prove that furnishing beverage was
negligent, if minor misrepresented himself this is evidence of non-negligence.
Open Container Prohibition: Yes.
PBTs: Allowed, not admissible as evidence.

Refusals to Submit:
10 days + 12 mos. lic. revoc. Work-restrictd lic. avail. after 6 mos., if 1st offense and no
death/injury occured.

.10 BAC:
10 day admin. lic. revoc.

Driving under Revoc. License:
Level 2, max $100, mand. 7 days-12 mos. jail, mand. 1 yr. lic. revoc.

---

If 1st offense and no serious injury occured, judge must review aggravating and mitigating factors:

| Aggravating include: | Mitigating include: |
|---|---|
| .20 BAC | undere .11 BAC |
| $500+ proper damage | driving safe/lawful other than DWI |
| personal injury | due to lawfully prescribed drug |
| eluded police | voluntary rehab. after charge |
| passed stopped school bus | |
| drove 30+ mph over limit | |

| | Penalties | Jail/CommSvc | LicRevoc/Rehab/Therapy | Other |
|---|---|---|---|---|
| 1st Offense (mitigating outweigh aggravating) | Level 5, max. $100, | | Mand. 24 hrs.-60 days jail, rehab., OR combination of 24 hrs jail, 24 hrs. comm. svc. w/in 30 days, 30 days lic. revoc., rehab. | |

134

| 1st Offense (counterbalanced) | Level 4, max. $250, | Mand. 48 hrs.-120 days jail, rehab., <u>OR</u> combination of 48 hrs. jail, 48 hrs. comm. svc. w/in 60 days, 60 days lic. revoc., rehab. | |
|---|---|---|---|
| 1st Offense (aggravating outweigh mitigating) | Level 3, max. $500, | Mand. 72 hrs.-6 mos. jail, rehab., <u>OR</u> combination of 72 hrs. jail, 72 hrs. comm. svc. w/in 90 days, 90 days lic. revoc., rehab. | |
| 2nd Offense w/in 7 yrs. or if 1st Offense/serious injury | Level 2, max. $1000, | Mand. 7 days-12 mos. jail, | Rehab, mand. 1 yr. lic. revoc. if serious injury. Otherwise 2 yrs. hard lic. revoc., 2 yrs. restricted. |
| 3rd offense w/in 7 yrs, or if 2 out of 3: serious injury, driving under DWI revoc. lic., 2nd Offense | Level 1, max. $1000, | Mand. 7 days-12 mos. jail, | Rehab. Mand. 4 yrs. lic. revoc. (2 yrs. hard). |
| 3rd Offense w/in 5 yrs | Same as above 3rd offense, | | 3 yrs.-permanent lic. revoc. |
| If death occurs | Class 1 felony, | | 3 yrs.-permanent lic. revoc. |

**Miscellaneous:**
  <u>Roadblocks</u> allowed by statute, plan must be developed in advance.

  <u>Pre-trial release of impaired driver:</u>
  Held in custody until no longer impaired, or if can be released to sober responsible adult.


## NORTH DAKOTA

<u>1984 Legislation:</u>
  **None; did not meet.**

**Per Se:** .10
**Drinking Age:** 21 yrs.
**Dram Shop Law:** NDCC5-01-06, recently revised (1983) to also allow damages if death occurs.
**Open Container Prohibition:** $20 fine.
**Section 408 Funds:** Received $387,264 Alcohol/Traffic Safety Grant (Basic and Supplemental).
**PBTs:** Allowed.

**Refusals to Submit:**
  1 yr. admin. lic. revoc., admissible as evidence.

**Driving under Revoc. License:**
  Class B misdemeanor, mand. 15 days jail, mand. fine (amount not specified). Possible m.v. plates impounded. Minimum 6 mos.-double original lic. revoc.

**.10 BAC Administrative License Revocation (separate from criminal disposition):**
  1st Offense: 90 days lic. revoc., 30 days hard.
  2nd Offense: 1 yr. hard. lic. revoc.

| | Penalties | Jail/CommSvc | LicRevoc/Rehab/Therapy | Other |
|---|---|---|---|---|
| 1st Offense | Class B misdemeanor, min. mand. $250. | | Rehab. | In-patient rehab. can be credited against jail sentence. |

| 2nd Offense w/in 5 yrs. | Class B misdemeanor, min. mand. $500 | Mand. 4 days jail (at least 48 hrs. consecutive) or 10 days comm. svc. | Rehab. | | In-patient rehab. can be credited against jail sentence. |
|---|---|---|---|---|---|
| 3rd Offense w/in 5 yrs. | Class A misdemeanor, mand. $1000 | Mand. 60 days jail (48 hrs. must be consecutive) | Rehab. | | In-patient rehab. can be credited against jail sentence. |
| 4th Offense w/in 7 yrs. | Class A misdemeanor, mand. $1000. | Mand. 180 days jail (48 hrs. must be consecutive). | | | In-patient rehab. can be credited against jail sentence. |
| If death occurs | Manslaughter or negligent homicide | Mand. 1 yr. jail | Mand. 1 yr. hard lic. revoc. | | In-patient rehab. can be credited against jail sentence. |

Miscellaneous:
  Failure to complete rehab:
    1st Failure:  Additional 180 days lic. revoc.
    2nd Failure:  Additional 1 yr. lic. revoc.
    Work-restricted lic. avail. for both after 7 days.


# OHIO

1984 Legislation:
  SB74 - Allows 19 yr. olds to serve distilled spirits in capacity of waiter/waitress, but not as bartender.

Per Se:  .10
Drinking Age:  19 yrs. for beer, 21 yrs. for wine/spirits.
Dram Shop Law:  none, except illegal to sell to intoxicated person, and can sue restaurant if damages occured on premises but not DWI.

Refusals to Submit or .10 BAC:
  Administratively imposed but, if plead guilty or convicted on DWI this revoc is terminated.  1 yr. lic. revoc., work restricted lic. avail.  If defendent appeals and loses, must pay cost of hearing.

Driving under Revoc. License:
  1st degree misdemeanor max. $500 and/or 1 yr. jail, additional lic. revoc. and possible vehicle impoundment.

| | Penalties | Jail/CommSvc | LicRevoc/Rehab/Therapy | Other |
|---|---|---|---|---|
| 1st Offense | $150-1000, | Mand. 3 days jail (being interpreted as 3 days in-house rehab.) | Mand. 60 days-3 yrs. lic revoc. (work-restricted lic. avail.), rehab. | |
| 2nd Offense w/in 5 yrs. | $150-1000, | Mand. 10 consecutive days jail. | Mand. 120 days-5 yrs. lkic. revoc. (work-restricted lic. avail.), rehab. | |

| 3rd Offense w/in 5 yrs. | $150-1000, | Mand. 30 consecutive days jail. | 180 days-50 yrs. lic. revoc. (work-restricted lic. not avail. until after 180 days), rehab. | |
|---|---|---|---|---|
| Vehicular Homicide - 1st Offense | 1st degree misdemeanor, no probation. | | Permanent lic. revoc. | |
| Vehicular Homicide - 2nd Offense | 4th degree felony, no probation. | | | |
| Aggravated Vehicular Homicide - 1st Offense | 3rd degree felony. | | Permanent lic. revoc. | |
| Aggravated Vehicular Homicide - 2nd Offense | No probation. | | | |

## OAKLAHOMA

### 1984 Legislation:

SB403 - Increases fee from $50 to $75 for DUI school.

HB1034 - Increases mand. lic. revoc. from 2 yrs. to 3 yrs. for 3rd offenders. Increases penalties for driving under DUI revoc. lic. from $100-500 and 10 days-2 mos. jail to min. $500 and 60 days-1 yr. jail. Discusses treatment/assessment program.

HB1432 - Refusal to submit is admissible as evidence.

Per Se: .10
Drinking Age: 21 yrs.
Dram Shop Law: No statute, although illegal to sell to intoxicated person.
Open Container Prohibition: $50-250, max. 6 mos. jail.

Refusals to Submit:
   90 days admin. lic. revoc., admissible as evidence.

Driving under Revoc. License (due to .10 or prior refusal):
   $100-500, 10 days-2 mos. jail.

| | Penalties | Jail/CommSvc | LicRevoc/Rehab/Therapy | Other |
|---|---|---|---|---|
| 1st Offense | Misdemeanor, max. $1000 | 10 days-1 yr. jail | Mand. 6 mos. lic. revoc. | |
| 1st Offense w/ injury | Misdemeanor, max. $2500 | 90 days-1 yr. jail | Mand. 6 mos. lic. revoc. | |
| 2nd Offense | Felony, max $2500 | 1-5 yrs. jail | Mand. 1 yr. lic. revoc. | |
| 2nd Offense w/ injury | Felony, max. $5000 | 1-5 yrs. jail | Mand. 1 yr. lic. revoc. | |

| 3rd Offense | Felony, max. $2500 | 1-5 yrs. jail | Mand. 3 yr. lic. revoc. (new) | |
| Negligent Homicide | $100-1000 | Max. 1 yr. jail | Mand. 6 mos. lic. revoc. | |

Miscellaneous:

If defendent pleads guilty, no contest, or convicted before judgement entered, judge can suspend execution of sentence upon condition that rehab. be completed.


## OREGON

1984 Legislation:
None; did not meet.

Per Se: .08
Drinking Age: 21 yrs.
Dram Shop Law: Revamped in 1979, liability extends to tavern-keepers and private hosts if defendent was visibly intoxicated. Defendent cannot recover, only 3rd party can recover (ORS 30.950).
Open Container Prohibition: Class B misdemeanor, max. $250.

Refusals to Submit (administratively imposed, admissible as evidence):
1st refusal: 1 yr. lic. revoc., 90 days hard.
2nd refusal: 3 yrs. lic. revoc., 1 yr. hard.

.08 BAC Administrative Penalties (separate from criminal disposition):
1st Offense: 90 days lic. revoc., 30 days hard.
2nd Offense: 1 yr. lic. revoc., 90 days hard.

Driving under Revoc. License due to Prior Homicide/Assault Charge:
Class C Felony, max. $100,000, 5 yrs. state prison.

Driving under Revoc. License due to Prior Refusal:
Class F misdemeanor.

Youth Offender Legislation for any alcohol-related offense (does not have to be DWI):
90 days lic. revoc. and 1 yr. admin. lic. revoc. or until age 17, whichever is longer.

| | Penalties | Jail/CommSvc | LicRevoc/Rehab/Therapy | Other |
| --- | --- | --- | --- | --- |
| 1st Offense, no crash | | | | Eligible for pre-trial diversion prog. $282, agree not to DWI, rehab + costs. |
| 1st Offense | Class A misdemeanor, max. $2500 | Mand. 48 hrs.-1 yr. jail or 80-250 hrs. comm. svc. | 1 yr. lic. revoc., work-restricted lic. avail. Mand. rehab. | |
| 2nd Offense w/in 5 yrs | Class A misdemeanor, max. $2500 | Mand. 48 hrs.-1 yr. jail or 80-250 hrs. comm. svc. | 3 yrs. lic. revoc., 90 days hard. Mand. rehab. | |
| 3rd Offense w/in 5 yrs. | Class A misdemeanor, max. $2500 | Mand. 48 hrs.-1 yr. jail or 80-250 hrs. comm. svc. | 3 yrs. lic. revoc., 1 yr. hard. Mand. rehab. | |
| If death occurs | | | Mand. 5 yrs. hard lic. revoc. | |

Miscellaneous:
Restitution can be recovered in DWI cases.
Requires pre-sentence investigation reports to include Victim Impact information.

## PENNSYLVANIA

<u>1984 Legislation:</u>
1 bill passed - <u>SB300</u> - DOT to distribute DWI penalty info. via renewels and new license applicants.
Remainder still pending in Committee, on recess until September 17, 1984.
<u>SB66</u> - Victim impact statement given, with defendent present when serious injury/death occcured.

<u>SB755</u> - Allows mand. jail to be served in municipal jail if available.  Additional $150 charge
   defendent must pay to municipality.

<u>SB178</u> - DMV to prepare listing for news media, of people with lic. revoc. due to DWI.

<u>SB1331</u> - $100 surcharge for Catastrophic Loss Trust Fund.

<u>SB138</u> - Court may order installation of alcohol safety interlock on car (tests reaction time or
   coordination of m.v. driver).

<u>SB1380</u> - Limits immunity of technician from civil liability while doing BAC test, unless behavior is
   intentional misconduct.

Per Se:  .10
Drinking Age:  21 yrs.
Dram Shop Law:  Yes, 47 §4-493
Open Container Prohibition:  Yes.
PBTs:  Allowed, refusal not admissible as evidence.

Refusals to Submit:
   12 mos. lic. revoc.

Driving under Revoc. License:
   $1000, 1 yr. jail, 6-12 mos. additional lic. revoc.

| | Penalties | Jail/CommSvc | LicRevoc/Rehab/Therapy | Other |
|---|---|---|---|---|
| 1st Offense | 2nd degree misdemeanor, min. $300, | Min. 48 hrs. jail, | Max. 6 mos. lic. revoc., pre-sentence assessment. | OR Accelerated Rehab Disposition Program if no injury/death. Counts as conviction, must pay own fees, mand. 30 days-12 mos. lic. revoc. restitution. |
| 2nd Offense w/in 7 yrs. | Min. $300, | Min. 30 days jail, | 1 yr. lic. revoc., pre-sentence assessment. | |
| 3rd Offense w/in 7 yrs. | Habitual offender, min. $300, | Min. 90 days jail, | 5 yr. lic. revoc, pre-sentence assessment. | |
| 4th Offense w/in 7 yrs. | Habitual offender, min. $300, | Min. 1 yr. jail, | Min. 5 yr. lic. revoc., pre-sentence assessment. | |
| Homicide by m.v. | 3rd degree felony, | Min. 3 yr. jail. | | |

139

## RHODE ISLAND

### 1984 Legislation:

S373 - Establishes flat maximum $500 fine for underage possession (was staggered from $100-500 according to prior offenses).

H7050 - Resolution asking U.S. Congress to ban alcohol advertising on radio and TV.

H7662 - Technical change clarifying administrative adjudication of drinking and driving (not DWI) offenses.

H7041 - Raises drinking age from 20 to 21 yrs.

Per Se: .10
Drinking Age: 21 yrs. (raised in 1984)
Open Container Prohibition: Only illegal for minors and extends to traveling with open or closed
                    containers.
Dram Shop Law: Limited; only if server was previously notified not to serve individual (not revised).
Section 408 Grant: Received $262,000 Alcohol/Traffic Safety Grant (Basic and Supplemental)
Procurement of Alcohol for Minors: Felony, max. $1000 &/or 6 mos. jail.

Drinking and Driving (not DWI):
    1st offense: max. $200 &/or max. 6 mos. lic. revoc.
    2nd offense: max. $500 &/or max. 1 yr. lic. revoc.

Refusals to Submit (Administrative Revocation):
    1st refusal: $200 minimum and $150 assessment, 10-60 hrs. comm. svc., 3-6 mos. lic. revoc.
    2nd refusal: $500 minimum and $150 assessment, 1-2 yr. lic. revoc.
    3rd refusal: $800 minimum and $150 assessment, 2-3 yrs. lic. revoc.

Driving under Revoc. License:
    1st Offense: Misdemeanor, $500, 10 days jail, additional 3 mos. lic. revoc.
    2nd Offense: $500, 6 mos.-1 yr. jail, additional 6 mos. lic. revoc.
    3rd Offense: felony, $1000, min. 1 yr. jail, permanent lic. revoc.

| | Penalties | Jail/CommSvc | Lic Revoc/Rehab/Therapy | Other |
|---|---|---|---|---|
| 1st Offense | $200,* | 10-60 hrs. comm. svc. &/or 1 yr. jail. | | |
| 2nd Offense | $500,* | 10 days jail. | 1-2 yrs. lic. revoc. and treatment ($150). | |
| 3rd Offense | $500,* | 6 mos.-1 yr. jail. | 2-3 yrs. lic. revoc. and treatment ($150). | |
| If death occurs - 1st Offense | Felony, $500-1000, | 6 mos.-10 yrs. jail, | 1 yr. lic. revoc. | |
| If death occurs - 2nd Offense | Felony, $800-5000, | 5-20 yrs. jail, | 3 yrs. lic. revoc. | |

* All penalties are minimum mandatory.

## SOUTH CAROLINA

<u>1984 Legislation:</u>
   <u>H2080</u> - Raises drinking age for beer/wine from 18 yrs. to 20 yrs. with grandfather clause.

   <u>S106</u> - Open container prohibition, misdemeanor, max $100 or max. 30 days jail.

Per Se:  none.
Drinking Age:  20 yrs. for beer/wine (new), 21 yrs. for distilled spirits.
Dram Shop Law:  None, except illegal to sell to intoxicated persons.
Open Container Prohibition:  New, see <u>S106</u>.

Refusals to Submit:
   90 day lic. revoc.

Driving under Revoc. License:
   1st Offense:  $100 or 30 days jail, additional revocation.
   2nd Offense:  $500 and/or max. 60 day jail, additional lic. revoc.
   3rd Offense:  45 days-6 mos. jail, additional lic. revoc.

|  | Penalties | Jail/CommSvc | LicRevoc/Rehab/Therapy | Other |
|---|---|---|---|---|
| 1st Offense | Mand. $200, | Mand. 48 hrs.-30 days jail (comm. svc. can be substituted for jail). | 6 mos. lic. revoc. | |
| 2nd Offense w/in 5 yrs. | Min. $1000. | Mand. 48 hrs. jail or 10 days comm. svc. | 1 yr. lic. revoc., restricted lic. avail. if enroll in ASAP. | |
| 3rd Offense w/in 5 yrs. | Min $2000, | Mand. 60 days-3 yrs. jail. | 2 yr. lic. revoc., restricted lic. avail. if enroll in ASAP. | |
| 4th Offense w/in 5 yrs. | Min. $3000, | Mand. 90 days-4 yrs. jail. | 3 yr. lic. revoc., restricted lic. avail. if enroll in ASAP. | |
| 5th Offense w/in 5 yrs. | | 1-5 yrs. jail. | 5 yr.-perm. lic. revoc., restricted lic. avail. if enroll in ASAP. | |
| DWI-Great bodily injury | Felony, mand. $5000-10,000, | Mand. 30 days-1 yr. jail. | | |
| DWI-Death | Felony, mand. $10,000-$25,000 , | Mand. 1-15 yrs. jail. | | |

Miscellaneous:
   Names/Addresses of all DWI's released to public each month.

## SOUTH DAKOTA

<u>1984 Legislation:</u>
   <u>HB1026</u> - Raises drinking age for 3.2 beer from 18 yrs. to 19 yrs.

Per Se:  .10
Drinking Age:  19 yrs. for 3.2 beer, 21 yrs. for everything else.
Dram Shop Law:  No specific statute, except illegal to sell to intoxicated persons. Some case law to
            support liability of vendor under this statute.
Open Container Prohibition:  Class 2 misdemeanor.

Refusals to Submit:
   Administratively imposed but penalty can be canceled if plead guilty to criminal charges before
   revoc. order is issued. Refusal admissible into evidence. Work restricted lic available.
   1 yr. lic. revoc.

## *Drinking and Driving*

Driving under Revoc. License:
  Class 2 misdemeanor, $100 and/or 30 days jail.

|  | Penalties | Jail/CommSvc | LicRevoc/Rehab/Therapy | Other |
|---|---|---|---|---|
| 1st Offense | Class 1 misdemeanor, max. $1000 | &/OR 1 yr. jail. | 30 day-1 yr. lic. revoc., work-restricted lic. avail. | |
| 2nd Offense w/in 5 yrs | Class 1 misdemeanor, max. $1000 | &/OR 1 yr. jail. | Mand. 1 yr. hard lic. revoc. | |
| 2nd Offense DWI & driving under revoked lic. | | Mand. 3 days jail. | | |
| 3rd Offense w/in 5 yrs. | Class 6 felony, $2000 | &/OR 2 yrs. jail. | Mand. 1 yr.-permanent hard lic. revoc. | |
| 3rd Offense DWI & driving under revoked lic. | | Mand. 10 days jail. | | |
| Vehicular homicide (while DWII) | Class 4 felony, $10,000 | &/OR 2 yrs. jail. | | |

Miscellaneous:
  <u>Prosecutor must state, or record, reasons</u> for reducing or dismissing .10 BAC chargeable offense.


## TENNESSEE

<u>1984 Legislation:</u>

  <u>SB4 (PC 1005)</u> - Raises drinking age to 21 yrs. Exempts active duty military personnel. Exempts 18-19 yr. olds accompanied by parents/legal guardians, however, parents/l.g. are civilly liable for damages caused.

  <u>HB1633 (PC 695)</u> - Driver must be told that refusal to submit to BAC test will result in license suspension.

  <u>SB1598 (PC 653)</u> - Relates to fees for drug analysis.

  <u>HB1402 (PC 597)</u> - Technical amendment relating to fees collected for BAC tests.

Per Se: none.
Drinking Age: 21 yrs. (new, see above)
Open Container Prohibition: none
Dram Shop Law: None, nor is there any prohibition against selling to intoxicated persons.

Refusals to Submit (administratively imposed):
  License revoked, no specific penalty set forth in statute.

Driving under Revoc. License:
  Illegal, no specific penalty set forth in statute. Unless habitual offender, then felony, max. $1000, in addition to other penalty set forth for felonies.

| | Penalties | Jail/CommSvc | LicRevoc/Rehab/Therapy | Other |
|---|---|---|---|---|
| 1st Offense | $250-500.* | 48 hrs.-1 yr. jail.* (48 hrs. can be served on weekends, remaining jail time, if any, can be satisfied by comm. svc. work.*) | 1 yr. lic. revoc., restricted lic. avail. | DUI school. |
| 2nd Offense w/in 10 yrs. | $500-2500,* | 45 days-1 yr. jail. | 2 yr. lic. revoc., rehab. | Restitution for injuries/ losses. |
| 3rd Offense w/in 10 yrs. | $1000-5000,* | 120 days-1 yr. jail. | 3-10 yr. lic. revoc., rehab. | Restitution. |
| Habitual Offender( 3 or more offenses w/in 3 yr. period.) | 3 yrs.-permanent lic. revoc. in addition to other penalties. | | | |

* All penalties are minimum mandatory.

Miscellaneous:
Portion of fine money returned to county for jail costs.
$10 BAC charge earmarked to each county to cover costs.


# TEXAS

__1984 Legislation:__
None; did not meet.

Per Se: .10
Drinking Age: 19 yrs.
Dram Shop Law: No specific statute giving right of action against 3rd party. There is a statute prohibiting sales to intoxicated persons.
Open Container Prohibition: none.

Refusals to Submit:
Admissible as evidence. Administratively imposed although lic. revoc period would be credited against any criminal DWI conviction (would run concurrently, not separately).
90 day lic. revoc.

Driving under Revoc. License:
Misdemeanor, $25-500 and 72 hrs.-6 mos. jail.

If allow m.v. to be used by DWI revoc. lic. holder:
Class B. misdemeanor, max. $1000 adn 180 days jail.

Youth Offender Legislation:
Between 14-17 yrs. old, if caught DWI, misdemeanor, max. $100 fine.

| | Penalties | Jail/CommSvc | LicRevoc/Rehab/Therapy | Other |
|---|---|---|---|---|
| 1st Offense | $100-2000. | 72 hrs.-2 yrs. jail. | 90-365 days lic. suspension | OR probation assessment (if county has funds) and rehab. |

| | | | | |
|---|---|---|---|---|
| 2nd Offense w/in 10 yrs. | $300-2000. | 15 days-2 yrs. jail. | 180 days lic. revoc. | OR probation and mand. 72 hrs. jail, and assessment (if county has funds) and rehab. |
| 3rd Offense w/in 10 yrs. | $500-2000. | 30 days-5 yrs. jail. | 180 days-2 yrs. lic revoc. | OR probation, mand. 10 days jail and assessment (if county has funds) and rehab. |
| If bodily injury | Additional $500 | AND additional 60 days jail. | | OR probation, mand 30 days jail, assessment (if county has funds) and rehab. |

Miscellaneous:
  3 yr. insurance premium surcharge per DWI offense.
  Mandates videotaping of DWI arrests in certain counties. Refusal to be videotaped is admissible as evidence.

# UTAH

1984 Legislation:
  HB125 - Allows impounded vehicle to be released if another registered owner is present at time of arrest.

Per Se: .08
Drinking Age: 21 yrs.
Dram Shop Law: No statute, except illegal to sell to intoxicated persons.
Open Container Prohibition: Exists.
Section 408 Grant: Received $383,915 Alcohol/Traffic Safety Grant (Basic and Supplemental).

Refusals to Submit or .08 BAC:
  Admissible, 1 yr. admin. lic. revoc. and $25 reinstatement. Possible vehicle impoundment.

Driving under DWI Revoc. License:
  $299-1000 and/or max. 1 yr. jail. Double orig. lic. revoc. period.

| | Penalties | Jail/CommSvc | LicRevoc/Rehab/Therapy | Other |
|---|---|---|---|---|
| 1st Offense | $299 and/or min. 60 days jail. | Mand. 48 hrs.-10 days drunk tank jail or 2-10 days comm. svc. | 90 days hard lic. revoc. | Mand. assessment and educ. |
| 2nd Offense w/in 5 yrs. | $299 and/or min. 60 days jail. | Mand. 48 hrs-10 days drunk tank jail or 10-30 days comm. svc. | 1 yr. hard lic. revoc. | Mand. assessment and educ. |

| 3rd Offense w/in 5 yrs. | $299 and/or min. 60 days jail. | Mand. 30-90 days drunk tank jail, or 30-90 days comm. svc. | 1 yr. hard lic. revoc. | Mand. assessment, educ. and rehab. |
|---|---|---|---|---|
| Bodily Injury | Max. $1000 and 1 yr. jail. | | | |
| Homicide by m.v. | 3rd degree felony. | | | |

# VERMONT

**1984 Legislation:**
HB387 (ACT 134) - Increases fines, including maximum assessment charged for rehab. from $125 to $175. Simplifies jail and license revocation penalties by deleting either/or options relating to rehab. Adds mandatory 48 hr. jail or 10 day community service for 2nd offenders. Adds mandatory therapy (in addition to rehab.) for repeat offenders.

Per Se: .10
Drinking Age: 18 yrs.
Dram Shop Law: Yes; Ch. 17, Title 7 §501.
Open Container Prohibition: None.
Admin. Lic. Revoc.: No, but if plead not guilty to DWI, judge can revoke license as condition of pre-trial release.
PBTs: Allowed, but not admissible as evidence.

Refusals to Submit (not administrative revocation):
  1st refusal:  6 mos. lic. revoc. & rehab. (was  1 yr. or 6 mos. & rehab.).
  2nd refusal: 18 mos. lic. revoc. & rehab. & therapy (was 18 mos. & rehab.).
  3rd refusal:  3 yrs. lic. revoc. & rehab. & therapy (was 6 yrs. or 3 yrs. & rehab.).
  4th refusal:  6 yrs. lic. revoc. & rehab. (new).
  4th refusal w/in 15 yrs.: Permanent lic. revoc.

Driving under Revoc. License:
  1st Offense:  $500 &/or 30 days jail
  2nd Offense:  $500 &/or 90 days jail
  3rd Offense:  $1000 &/or 6 mos. jail
  4th Offense:  $1000 &/or 2 yrs. jail

| | Penalties | Jail/CommSvc | LicRev/Rehab/Therapy | Other |
|---|---|---|---|---|
| 1st Offense | $200-750 (was $50-500), | And/or max. 1 yr. jail (was max. 2 yrs. jail) | 90 days lic. revoc. & rehab. (was 1 yr. lic. revoc. OR 90 days & rehab.). 1 yr. lic. revoc. & rehab. if fatality occured. | |
| 2nd Offense w/in 5 yrs. | $250-1000 (was $500) | Mand. 48 hrs.-1 yr. jail or 10 days comm. svc. (new; was max. 2 mos.-2 yrs. jail). | 18 mos. lic. revoc. & rehab. & therapy (paid for by defendant) (was 3 yrs. lic. revoc. OR 18 mos. & rehab.) | |
| 3rd Offense w/in 15 yrs. | $500-1500 (was $500) | Mand. 48 hrs.-1 yr. jail or 10 days comm. svc. (new; was 2 mos.-2 yrs. jail). | 3 yrs. lic. revoc. & rehab. & therapy. | If lic. is suspended for 3 yrs.+, can apply for reinstatement after 2 yrs. if defendant can prove total abstinance from drugs &/or alcohol. |
| 4th Offense w/in 15 yrs. | Same penalties as 2nd and 3rd offense except permanent lic. revoc. | | | If death/injury can also prosecute for manslaughter |
| If death or injury | Max. $3000, | 1-15 yrs jail. | | |

# *Drinking and Driving*

## VIRGINIA

1984 Legislation:

S306 (ch623) - Increases penalties for refusal to submit to BAC test. Stipulates that revoc. period does not begin until lic is surrendered to Court or DMV.

H958 (ch666) - Establishes .15 per se, allows police officer, not defendant, to choose type of BAC test given.

Per Se: .15 (new)
Drinking Age: 19 yrs. for beer, 21 yrs. for wine and spirits.
Dram Shop Law: none, except misdemeanor to sell to intoxicated person (§4-1112).
Open Container Prohibition: none

Refusals to Submit to BAC test (imposed by Court but independent of criminal sanctions):
1st refusal:  6 mos. (was 90 days) lic. revoc.
2nd refusal:  1 yr. (was 6 mos.) lic. revoc.

Driving under Revoc. License:
Misdemeanor, max. $500, 10 days-6 mos. jail.

| | Penalties | Jail/CommSvc | LicRevoc/Rehab/Therapy | Other |
|---|---|---|---|---|
| 1st Offense | | | 6 mos. lic. revoc., may be suspended if rehab. | |
| 2nd Offense w/in 5 yrs. | $200-1000, | Mand. 48 hrs.-1 yr. jail. | Mand. 2-3 yr. lic. revoc. and rehab. | |
| 2nd Offense w/in 5-10 yrs. | $200-1000, | 1 mo.-1 yr. jail. | Mand. 1-3 yr. lic. revoc. and rehab. | |
| 3rd Offense w/in 5 yrs. | $500-1000, | Mand. 30 days-1 yr. jail. | Perm. lic. revoc., ineligible to participate in special rehab. program to regain lic. quickly. | |
| 3rd Offense w/in 5-10 yrs. | $500-1000, | Mand. 10 days-1 yr. jail. | Perm. lic. revoc., ineligible to participate in special rehab. program to regain lic. quickly. | |
| 3rd Offense w/in 10 yrs. | $500-1000, | 2 mos.-1 yr. jail. | Perm. lic. revoc., ineligible to participate in special rehab. program to regain lic. quickly. | |

## WASHINGTON

1984 Legislation:

HB1582 -- $3 million appropriation to counties to help pay enforcement (primarily adjudication) of DWI. Needed because many cities are refusing to prosecute because of state Supreme Court case requiring speedy jury trials be offered to traffic infraction violators (DWI). The cases are being heard at county level instead.

SB4362 - Exempts vehicles for hire from open container law  Illegal to mislabel alcohol container or add alcohol to non-alcoholic container while in m.v.

Per Se: .10
Drinking Age: 21 yrs.
Dram Shop Law: Illegal to sell to intoxicated person, but no clear 3rd party liability established.
Open Container Prohibition: Yes.

146

Refusals to Submit:
    Criminal and admin. lic. revoc. penalties run concurrently; longer period to prevail.
    1st refusal:  1 yr. admin. lic. revoc.
    2nd refusal:  2 yrs. admin. lic. revoc.

Admin. Lic. Revoc. for .10:
    Criminal and admin. lic. revoc. penalties run concurrently; longer period to prevail.
    1st Offense:  90 days admin. lic. revoc.
    2nd Offense w/in 5 yrs.:  1 yr. admin. lic. revoc.
    3rd Offense w/in 5 yrs.:  2 yrs. admin. lic. revoc.

DWI and Driving under DWI/Revoc. License:
    Mand. $200, mand. 90 days jail, diagnostic evaluation and rehab., additional 180 days-1 yr. jail if
    terms of sentence are violated.
    Additional assessment of 25% of fine.  Monies go to fund driver Alcohol Services Programs.

Youthful Offender Legislation:
    If under 19 yrs. old and charges with DWI license suspended until 19th birthday, or for 90 days,
    whichever is longer.

| | Penalties | Jail/CommSvc | LicRevoc/Rehab/Therapy | Other |
|---|---|---|---|---|
| 1st Offense | Max. $750, | Mand. 24 hrs.-1 yr. jail, unless judge finds jail poses physical/ mental risk. | 60 days hard lic. revoc., 30 days restricted. Diagnostic evaluation and rehab. | |
| 2nd Offense w/in 5 yrs. | Max. $1500, | Mand. 7 days-1 yr. jail, unless judge finds jail poses physical/ mental risk. | 1 yr. hard lic. revoc. Diagnostic evaluation and rehab. | Additional 180 days-1 yr. jail levied if terms of sentence are violated. |
| 3rd Offense w/in 5 yrs. | Max. $1500, | Mand. 7 days-1 yr. jail, unless judge finds jail poses physical/ mental risk. | 2 yrs. hard lic. revoc. Diagnostic evaluation and rehab. | Additional 180 days-1 yr. jail levied if terms of sentence are violated. |

## WASHINGTON, D.C.

1984 Legislation:
    Nothing passed, two bills pending, both will die.
    5-85 - Raises drinking age to 21 yrs.
    5-22 - Adds 48 hrs. jail or 10 days community service for repeat offenders (attempts to qualify for
    the Sec. 408 grants).

Per Se:  .10
Drinking Age:  18 yrs. for beer/wine, 21 yrs. for distilled spirits.
Dram Shop Law:  Illegal to sell to intoxicated persons.  Case law supports 3rd party (dram shop)
                liability.  Specifically forbids dram shop liability of private host.  25§121
Open Container Prohibition:  None.

Refusals to Submit:
    12 mos. lic. revoc. admissible as evidence.

Driving under Revoc. License:
    Max. $5000 and/or max. 1 yr. jail.

| | Penalties | Jail/CommSvc | LicRevoc/Rehab/Therapy | Other |
|---|---|---|---|---|
| 1st Offense .10 | Max $300, | 90 days jail, | Yes. | OR probation if BAC less than .20, rehab, must pay own fees. |
| 2nd Offense w/in 5 yrs. .10 | $5000 | And/or 1 yr. jail. | Yes. | |
| 3rd Offense w/in 5 yrs. .10 | $10,000 | And/or 1 yr. jail. | Yes. | |
| 1st Offense DUI (less than .10) | $300 | And/or 30 days jail. | Yes. | |
| 2nd Offense DUI w/in 5 yrs. | $300 | And/or 90 days jail. | Yes. | |
| 3rd Offense DUI w/in 5 yrs. | Max. $5000 | Max. 1 yr. jail. | Yes. | |
| Negligent homicide | Felony, max. $5,000 | And/or 5 yrs. jail | Yes. | |

License can be revoked for all offenses, no statutory limits given.

If BAC is .10+, practice is to suspend lic. pending outcome of criminal proceedings.

Miscellaneous:
Implied consent law provides that 2 tests can be given, both chosen by police.

All fine monies go to Ofc. of Alcohol Countermeasures.

## WEST VIRGINIA

1984 Legislation:
No legislation passed this year.

Per Se: No .10 criminal per se. .10 prima facie and .10 administrative per se (for license revocations only).
Drinking Age: 19 yrs. for residents, 21 yrs. for non-residents.
PBTs: Allowed but not admissible as evidence.
Dram Shop Law: Illegal to sell to intoxicated person but no dram shop liability against seller (§60.3-22).
Open Container Prohibition: Misdemeanor $5-100 and/or max. 60 days jail.

Refusals to Submit (Administratively imposed but to run concurrently with any other sentence imposed.):
1st refusal: 1 yr. admin. lic. revoc.
2nd refusal: 5-10 yrs. admin. lic. revoc.
3rd refusal: 10 yrs-permanent admin. lic. revoc.

Driving under Revoc. License & Refusing BAC (both):
1st Offense: misdemeanor, $100-500, 48 hrs.-6 mos. jail.
2nd Offense: misdemeanor, $1000-3000, 6 mos.-1 yr. jail.
3rd Offense: felony, $3000-5000, 1-3 yrs. jail.

| | Penalties | Jail/CommSvc | LicRevoc/Rehab/Therapy | Other |
|---|---|---|---|---|
| 1st Offense | Misdemeanor, $100-500. | Mand. 24 hrs.-6 mos. jail or comm. svc. | 6 mos. admin. lic. revoc. or 90 days & rehab. | |
| 1st Offense w/ injury | Misdemeanor, $200-1000. | Mand. 24 hrs.-6 mos. jail or comm. svc. | 2 yrs. admin. lic. revoc. or 1 yr. & rehab. | |
| 1st Offense w/ death | Misdemeanor, $500-1000. | Mand. 90 days-1 yr. jail or comm. svc. | 5 yrs. admin. lic. revoc. or 2-1/2 yrs. and rehab. | |
| 1st Offense of giving car to DUI driver | Misdemeanor, $100-500, | Max. 6 mos. jail. | 6 mos. admin. lic. revoc. or 90 days and rehab. | |
| 2nd Offense | Misdemeanor, $1000-3000. | Mand. 6 mos.-1 yr. jail or comm. svc. | 10 yrs.-permanent admin. lic. revoc. or 5 yrs. and rehab. | |
| 3rd Offense | Felony, $3000-5000. | Mand. 1-3 yrs. jail or comm. svc. | Permanent lic. revoc. or 10 yrs. and rehab. | |
| If DUI and death occurs due to DUI | Felony, $100-3000. | Mand. 1-3 yr. jail or comm. svc. | 10 yrs. lic. revoc. or 5 yrs. and rehab. | |

Miscellaneous:
Blood tests required for all drivers and pedestrians killed in m.v. crashes. Info can only be used for statistical purposes.

## WISCONSIN

1984 Legislation:
   AB169 (Act 472) - Expands restrictions on consumption of alcohol by minors by specifically forbidding adults to allow underage consumption on premises owned or under control of the adult. Exemption for religious services.

   SB232 (ACT 535 - Allows conviction of similar local ordinance of driving under revoked license to be considered as prior offense. Increases penalties for habitual offenders (4 or more offenses). Other technical changes.

Per Se: .10
Drinking Age: 19 yrs. (raised in 1983).
Open Container Prohibition: Yes.
Dram Shop Law: Limited; only if server was previously notified not to serve individual (not revised; 176.30).
PBTs: Allowed, not admissible as evidence.

Refusals to Submit (Administrative Revocation):
   1st refusal: 6 mos. lic. revoc. and assessment, 15 days hard revoc. included.
   2nd refusal: 1 yr. lic. revoc. and assessment, 60 days hard revoc. included.
   3rd refusal: 2 yr. lic. revoc. and assessment, 90 days hard revoc. included.

Driving under Revoc. License:
   1st Offense: $150-600, max. 6 mos. jail, 6 mos. hard lic. revoc.
   2nd Offense: $300-1000, 10 days-6 mos. jail, 6 mos. hard lic. revoc.
   3rd Offense: $1000-2000, 30 days-9 mos. jail, 6 mos. hard lic. revoc.
   4th Offense: $1500,2000, 60 days-1 yr. jail, 6 mos. hard lic. revoc.
   5th Offense: $2000-2500, 6 mos.-1 yr. jail, 6 mos. hard lic. revoc.

| | Penalties | Jail/CommSvc | LicRevoc/Rehab/Therapy | Other |
|---|---|---|---|---|
| 1st Offense | $150-300.* | | 3-6 mos. lic. revoc. Work restricted lic. avail. Alcohol assessment & necessary treatment. | |
| 2nd Offense | $300-1000,* | 5 days-6 mos. jail. | 6-12 mos.lic. revoc.; 30 days hard. Alcohol assessment & necessary treatment. | |

| | | | | |
|---|---|---|---|---|
| 3rd Offense | $600-2000,* | 30 days-1 yr. jail. | 1-2 yr. lic. revoc.; 60 days hard. | |
| 4th Offense | Habitual offender $5000,* | 180 days jail. | Lic. revoc. | |
| If injury while OWI | $300-2000,* | 30 day-1 yr. jail. | 1-2 yrs. lic. revoc.; 60 days hard. Alcohol assessment & necessary treatment. | |
| If great bodily harm while OWI | Max. $10,000, max. 2 yrs. jail.* | | 2 yr. lic. revoc.; 120 days hard. | |
| Homicide while OWI | Same as great bodily harm except max. 5 yrs. jail and 5 yrs. lic. revoc.* | | | |

\* All penalties are minimum mandatory.

Miscellaneous:
  Mandatory $150 highway assessment added to all OWI's and refusals.
  Restrictions on plea bargains, prosecutor must apply to court for permission.

## WYOMING

1984 Legislation:
  SF46 (CH. 41) - Provides for admin. lic. revoc. if arrested for DWI. Lic. surrendered to police at time of stop. Changes lic. revoc. period for 3rd Offender from permanent to 3 yrs.

Per Se: No per se, .10 presumptive only.
Drinking Age: 19 yrs.
Dram Shop Law: Statute gives right of action only to those related to habitual drunkard who gave bar owner notice not to sell to that person (§12-5-502).
Open Container Prohibition: None.

Refusals to Submit:
  30 days lic. revoc., if hearing requested, revoc. stayed.

Driving under Suspended Lic.:
  Max. $750,, 6 mos. jail.

| | Penalties | Jail/CommSvc | LicRevoc/Rehab/Therapy | Other |
|---|---|---|---|---|
| 1st Offense | $750, | OR 6 mos. jail. | 3 mos. lic. revoc. | |
| 2nd Offense | $200-750, | Mand. 7 days-6 mos. jail, | 1 yr. lic. revoc. Rehab. | |
| 3rd Offense | $200-750, | Mand. 7 days-6 mos. jail, | 3 yrs. lic. revoc. (new) Rehab. | |
| Serious bodily injury - 1st Offense | Max. $5000, | and/or 1 yr. jail, | 2 yrs. lic. revoc. | |
| Serious bodily injury - 2nd Offense | Max. $5000, | 20 yrs. jail, | 2 yrs. lic. revoc. | |
| Homicide by M.V. | Felony, | Max 20 yrs. jail, | Permanent lic. revoc. | |

# Appendix B

## Driving Under the Influence Laws Around the World

This information has been drawn from various sources. Any incorrect statements are attributal to the sources. [42, 43]

### Algeria

A blood alcohol level of .08 percent is considered driving under the influence. Penalties range from two months to three years in jail and a fine.

### Australia

A BAC of .05 percent is evidence of intoxication. Random breath testing is done by the police. Possible imprisonment, with a fine of up to $600. The guilty parties' names may appear in the paper.

### Austria

A blood alcohol level of .08 percent is evidence of intoxication. It is determined with the breath test. Information on penalties was unavailable.

### Barbados

Any person who drives, or attempts to drive, or is in charge of a motor vehicle on a road while under the influence of alcohol or drugs to such an extent as to be incapable of having proper control of the vehicle is guilty of an offense.

### Belgium

A drunk driving conviction results when the BAC is .08 percent. Information on penalties was unavailable.

### Brazil

Drunk driving conviction relies solely on the testimony of the arresting officer. Information on penalties was unavailable.

### Bulgaria

A BAC of .03 percent is deemed driving under the influence which entails fines and possible incarceration. Information on penalties was unavailable.

### Canada

A blood alcohol of .08 percent determined by a breath test is evidence of intoxication. Refusing to take the test is punished by fines and imprisonment; the same punishment is applied for failing the test. Fines are up to $1000 and the possibility of six months in jail. A police officer must have reasonable and probable cause to administer a breath test. Licenses may be suspended for up to three years. Depending on the circumstances, jail sentences may be up to three years.

### Chile

The military government incarcerates a drunken driver for sixty-one to 541 days. If someone has been injured, the offender faces up to one and a half years in jail.

### Czechoslovakia

They forbid all drivers from drinking at all; a system patterned after the policies in effect in the Scandinavian countries. A blood alcohol of .03 percent is deemed driving under the influence and leads to a conviction. Information on penalties was unavailable.

### Denmark

A BAC of .08 to .12 percent will result in fines, as well as possible license suspension. Prison is possible with a second offense. Mandatory license suspension attaches to more serious violations and prison is a potential punishment if the blood alcohol level is above .15 percent. Breath tests are administered arbitrarily by the Danish police.

## Egypt
Like most Moslem countries, alcohol usage is prohibited and drunken driving cases are rare.

## Finland
Finland now has a two-tiered system of analyzing blood alcohol level for evidence of driving under the influence, similar to the Swedish DUI laws. Prior to the implementation of these laws, Finland's punishments were four years in prison for a simple offense and up to eight years if drunk driving resulted in a fatal accident. Now most sentences are three to six months in prison.

## France
A BAC of .08 percent leads to fines of up to $1,600. Licenses can be suspended for up to a lifetime if death or serious injury occurs. Random breath testing at prescribed roadblocks is common.

## Gabon
A BAC of .08 percent is deemed driving under the influence. Drivers are required to submit to a breath test whenever requested to do so by a competent authority.

## Germany (East)
A blood alcohol level of .03 percent is deemed driving under the influence and leads to a conviction. Information on penalties was unavailable.

## Germany (West)
A BAC level of .08 percent is deemed driving under the influence and can be punished by automatic license suspension for three months, with a maximum of one year in prison or fine. The police use roadblock checkpoints at random.

## Great Britain
The Road Safety Act of Great Britain states that any driver ordered by the police to take a breath test must do so. Refusal to take a breath test, blood test, or urine test is viewed as failure of the tests. A BAC of .08 percent or higher results in a fine of $240, license suspension for one year, and up to four months in jail. In severe cases a driver can be banned from the roads for life. Breath tests may be administered arbitrarily.

## Greece
A drunk driving conviction results if the BAC is .05 percent or higher. Information on penalties was not available.

## Hong Kong
A first offense in Hong Kong will result in a fine of $170 and six months in jail.

## Hungary
Breath tests are given, and where the test is deemed positive, a blood test is given two or three times if there is a discrepancy. Information on penalties was unavailable.

## Iceland

With BAC of .05 percent the person is presumed to be under the influence of alcohol. An upper limit of .12 percent BAC will usually result in imprisonment for a period of ten to twelve days.

## India

Drunk driving arrests are rare. Those convicted face six months in prison, $112 fine, or both.

## Ireland

A person is considered DUI when the BAC is .10 percent or higher, and the urine tests out at .135 percent or higher. Information on penalties was unavailable.

## Israel

A drinking and driving conviction may result in a two-year prison term.

## Italy

Italy permits testing for BAC only with the driver's consent. No level of tolerance has been established by the legislature or judicial authority. A drunk driving conviction basically relies solely on the testimony of the arresting officer. Information on penalties was unavailable.

## Japan

First offenders can face up to four months in jail and a $200 fine. Licenses are also revoked and can be returned only upon completion of a driving test one year later.

## Mexico

A drunk driving conviction relies solely on the arresting officer. Information on penalties was unavailable.

## Netherlands

A blood alcohol level of .05 percent and above is deemed DUI. The penalties are $2,500, license suspension for up to five years, and prison terms of up to three months. However, if someone is injured, the sentence is two years; three years if someone is killed. If the BAC test in the field is failed, another test may be taken at the police station. If the first test is failed and the second test is passed, the person is not prosecuted. Unlike Great Britain, the police must have reason to suspect a driver has consumed alcohol before testing.

## New Zealand

Breath tests are given wherein 500 micrograms of alcohol or more, or a BAC of .08 percent is deemed an offense. Information on penalties was unavailable.

## Norway

A blood alcohol level of .05 percent or higher is deemed DUI. Imprisonment and license suspension are swiftly accomplished. Roadblocks and breath testing are common. The people are very much aware of the law, due in part to the fast action of the authorities. The police are also authorized to check insurance papers at random. First-offense drunk driving results in three weeks in jail and license suspension for one year. In fatal accidents the license can be revoked for life.

**Poland**

With a BAC of .05 percent the person is presumed to be under the influence of alcohol. Information on penalties was unavailable.

**South Africa**

A first offense will cost $400, one year in jail, or both. Extremely intoxicated drivers face double penalties. Repeat offenders face up to 10 years in jail.

**South Korea**

Arrest includes an automatic two-month license suspension and conviction can bring a jail sentence of up to one year and a fine of $700.

**Soviet Union**

Drunk drivers are banned from the road for six months. Repeat offenders face stiffer punishments.

**Spain**

Spain has no prescribed limit of tolerance but breath samples are required and the results may be introduced as evidence if a drunk driving incident comes to court.

**Sweden**

Blood alcohol levels between .08 and 1.49 percent, and 1.50 percent or over will result in different punishments. These punishments range from heavy fines to relatively prompt jail sentences, which differentiates Sweden's procedures from those in the rest of the world. The Swedish people are well aware of these punishments and how swiftly the law works in DUI cases. However, in Sweden, as well as in Denmark, drivers must pay back the insurance company for any claims made against it by the heirs of those killed or injured. A first offense results in a fine proportionate to the driver's income and/or imprisonment up to six months. A high BAC usually results in jail time.

**Switzerland**

A blood alcohol level of .08 percent is deemed driving under the influence. Information on penalties was unavailable.

**Tunisia**

The law simply states that no one should drive while under the influence (a decree is to prescribe the level of alcohol in the blood above which a driver is to be deemed under the influence). Information on penalties was unavailable.

**Turkey**

A drunk driver is taken twenty miles from town and made to walk back under police escort.

**Uganda**

The prescribed limit for alcohol in the system is below .08 percent BAC. Information on penalties was unavailable.

**Yugoslavia**

A BAC level of .05 percent is presumed to be under the influence of alcohol. Information on penalties was unavailable.

# Glossary of Terms

| | |
|---|---|
| Alcohol Countermeasures: | Programs designed to deter the drunk driver. |
| BAC: | Blood alcohol concentration; amount of alcohol in the blood stream expressed as a percent. In most States, 0.10 percent (one-tenth of one percent) BAC or higher is under the influence of intoxicating liquor. Also referred to as blood alcohol content, blood alcohol level (BAL) or breath alcohol content. |
| Blood Alcohol Test: | Any chemical test of breath, blood, urine, or other bodily substance used to determine the concentration of alcohol in the blood. |
| Breath Testing Device: | An instrument which scientifically measures the amount of alcohol in the bloodstream by chemical analysis of the breath. |
| "Dram Shop" Laws: | Laws which state that those who dispense alcoholic beverages to intoxicated individuals may be held liable for subsequent injuries caused by such individuals. |
| DUI: | Driving under the influence or while intoxicated; operating or being in physical control of a vehicle while under the influence of intoxicating liquor. |
| Field Sobriety Test: | A roadside test used by police to help determine if a suspect is drunk. May include walking a straight line, touching fingers to the nose with the eyes closed, reciting the alphabet, étc. |
| Implied Consent Law: | A law in all States which stipulates that any person who operates a motor vehicle on the highways is presumed to have consented to be chemically tested for alcohol upon request by police, or risk license suspension. |
| PBT: | Preliminary breath tests: a roadside test by police using a portable breath-alcohol tester to measure a suspect's intoxication level. Results of this test may be used to establish probable cause for arrest. |
| Plea Bargaining: | The process by which a prosecutor and a defense attorney agree to reduce a given charge to an offense with lesser penalties in exchange for a guilty plea to the lesser offense by the defendant; for example, reducing a drunk driving charge to one of reckless driving. |
| Presumptive Laws: | Laws which state that if a specified level of alcohol is present in a driver's blood, the driver is presumed to have been driving under the influence or intoxicated. However, because the presumption is rebuttable, other evidence can be introduced by the defendant to disprove the allegation. |
| Illegal Per Se Laws: | Laws which make it an offense to operate a motor vehicle with a specified amount of alcohol in the blood. In States having such laws the specified amount of BAC is 0.10 percent. Rebuttable evidence is not considered relevant, except that the test was improperly administered. |
| Administrative Per Se Laws: | Laws which state that if a driver's blood alcohol concentration is in excess of a specific level (typically 0.10 percent), the State driver licensing agency may suspend the driver's license via administrative action which is independent of any court action related to a DUI charge. |
| Screening/Evaluation | A court-directed procedure used to determine a driver's level of involvement with alcohol for purposes of referral to education or treatment programs as appropriate. |

156

# Notes

1. "What Happens in High-speed Auto Smashups." National Council on Alcoholism – San Francisco Bay Area, 9-81, p. 1.

2. *Los Angeles Times,* Sports Section, 2-26-85, p. 2.

3. *San Francisco Chronicle,* 12-30-84, p. 2.

4. Editorial, *San Francisco Chronicle,* 1-1-85, p. 36.

5. *San Francisco Chronicle,* 12-30-84, p. 2.

6. Gallup Poll. The Gallup Organization, Inc. 53 Bank St., Princeton, N.J., 1983 and 1984.

7. Blomberg, R.D., and Preusser, D.F. *Drug Abuse and Driving Performance.*

8. Mayer, J., and Goldberg, J. "Alcohol Works Mysteriously on the Organs of the Body," Washington Post, Inc., 1982.

9. "The Way To Go," Kemper Group, Long Grove, Illinois, 1976, p. 2.

10. Ross, Laurence H. *Deterring the Drinking Driver: Legal Policy and Social Control.* Lexington, Massachusetts: D. C. Heath and Company, 1982.

11. R.E. Hagen et al., "An Evaluation of Alcohol Abuse Treatment as an Alternative to Driver's License Suspension or Revocation," p. 75.

12. R.E. Hagen et al., "Suspension and Revocation Effects on the DUI Offender," p. 68.

13. Ellingstad, V. S., and Struckman-Johnson, D. L. "Short-term Rehabilitation Study, Interim Analysis of STR Performance and Effectiveness," *Interim Report,* NHTSA, Washington, D.C., June, 1977.

14. "The Drunk Driver May Kill You," Allstate Insurance Companies, Northbrook, Illinois, pp. 10-18.

15. MADD, Student Packet, 1985, pp. 1-52.

16. Preferred Risk Mutual Insurance Co., "How Drinking Affects Drivers; Half-drunk Drivers are Dangerous Too," American Council of Alcohol Problems, Washington, D.C., May, 1979, pp. 1-4.

17. Felix, R. H. "Emotions and Your Driving," California Automobile Association, Traffic Safety Division, San Francisco, California, May, 1984, pp. 1-4.

18. *Marin Independent Journal,* May 24, 1985, p. A-10.

19. *San Francisco Examiner,* May 31, 1985, p. B-10.

20. Policy Update, National Safety Council, "1984 Drunk Driving Legislation Update, State and Federal Activity," Office of Federal Affairs, Washington, D.C., 1984.

21. "A Guide, Not a Guarantee," California Department of Motor Vehicles, January, 1984, p. 4.

22. J.C. Fell, *A Profile of Fatal Accidents Involving Alcohol.*

23. U.S. Department of Health, Education, and Welfare, "Young People and Alcohol," *Alcohol, Health, and Research World,* 1975, pp. 2-10.

24. Ibid, p. 4.

25. Ibid, p. 6.

26. Ibid, p. 7.

27. Ibid, p. 10.

28. "The Key to Recovery," National Council on Alcoholism – San Francisco Bay Area, 1984, pp. 1-2.

29. Alcoholics Anonymous, "44 Questions," World Services, Inc., New York, p. 11.

30. RID, "Will You Be The Next Victim of the Drunk Driver?" 1984, pp. 1-2.

31. MADD, op. cit., p. 32.

32. National Newsletter, MADD, Vol. 4, No. 2, Winter, 1984, p. 4.
33. Students Against Driving Drunk, "If We Dream It Can Be Done," 1985.
34. National Newsletter, op. cit., p. 2.
35. Patyk, Paula, "Believe Me, You Can Make a Difference," *Fifty Plus,* N.Y., May, 1983.
36. Ibid, p. 2.
37. RID, op. cit., p. 2.
38. MADD, op. cit., p. 32.
39. Students Against Driving Drunk, op. cit., p. 2.
40. "Help Stop Drunk Driving," California Trucking Association, 1984, pp. 1-2.
41. Patyk, op. cit., p. 4.
42. Most information on international drunk driving laws was obtained through the International Digest of Health Legislation, and from H. Lawrence Ross' study: "Deterrence of the Drinking Driver: an International Survey," published by the U.S. Department of Transportation, 1981.
43. "Drunk Driving Laws in Various Countries," Library of Congress Law Library reprint, 1983.

# Bibliography

Baker, S.P., and Spitz, W.U. "Age Effects and Autopsy Evidence of Disease in Fatally Injured Drivers." *Journal of the American Medical Association,* 1970. p. 214.

Blomberg, R.D., and Preusser, D.F. *Drug Abuse and Driving Performance.* Darien, Connecticut: Dunlap and Associates, Inc. October, 1972.

Ellingstad, V.S. and Struckman-Johnson, D.L. "Short-term Rehabilitation Study, Interim Analysis of STR Performance and Effectiveness." *Interim Report.* NHTSA, Washington, D.C. June, 1977.

Fell, J.C. *A Profile of Fatal Accidents Involving Alcohol.* Washington, D.C.: National Center for Statistics and Analysis. September, 1977.

Hagen, R.E., Williams, R.L., McConnell, E.J., and Fleming, C.W. "An Evaluation of Alcohol Abuse Treatment as an Alternative to Driver's License Suspension or Revocation," Sacramento: California Department of Motor Vehicles, 1978.

Hagen, R.E., McConnell, E.J., and Williams, R.L. "Suspension and Revocation Effects on the DUI Offender." Sacramento: California Department of Motor Vehicles, July, 1980.

National Highway Traffic Safety Administration, U.S. Department of Transportation, "To Promote Observance of National Drunk and Drugged Driving Week," December, 1984.

National Highway Traffic Safety Administration. "Facts on Alcohol and Highway Safety." Washington, D.C.: The Administration, 1983.

National Personal Transportation Survey, FHWA. Washington, D.C., 1977.

# Index

# ORDER FORM

## PARK WEST PUBLISHING COMPANY
## Post Office Box 1502, Sausalito, Calfiornia 94966

Please send me the following books

**SELF HYPNOSIS: A Method of Improving Your Life**

_____ copies ( $6.95 ea. )

**DRINKING & DRIVING: Know Your Limits and Liabilities**

_____ copies ( $5.95 ea. )

Name: _____

Address: _____

City/State/Zip: _____

*California Residents Please Add 6% Sales Tax.*

**Shipping:**
$2.00 per book. If paid in Canadian currency add three dollars per book, If *large* quantities of books are desired, contact Park West Publishing Co. for terms. (415) 435-1469.

# SELF-HYPNOSIS TAPES
## PARK WEST - P.O. BOX 1502
### Sausalito, CA 94965

*Cartridge or 8-Track*
**$9.98**

**EDUCATIONAL SERIES**
1 Memory
2 Self Hypnosis
3 Good Study Habits
4 Faster Reading
5 Concentration
6 Taking Exams

**FEAR SERIES**
7 Flying
8 Water
9 Driving
10 Death
11 Crowds
12 Heights
13 Closed In Places

**HABIT SERIES**
14 Stop Smoking
15 Weight Loss
16 Control Drinking Habits
17 Stop Thumb Sucking
18 Stop Nail Biting
19 Stop Bed Wetting
20 Stop Facial Tic

**PHYSICAL HEALTH SERIES**
21 Freedom From Allergies
22 Freedom From Acne
23 Recapture Youthful Vigor
24 Improving Vision
25 Healthy Teeth and Gums
26 Pleasant Dentistry
27 Lower High Blood Pressure
28 Relaxation
29 Migrain Relief
30 Stomach Problems
31 Stop Loss of Hair
32 Pain Relief
33 Arthritis Pain
34 Freedom From Drugs
35 Hearing Loss
36 Insomnia
37 Menstrual Problems
38 Operations - Before & After
39 Gaining Weight

**EMOTIONAL HEALTH SERIES**
40 Relieve Stress and Anxiety
41 Good Health
42 I Want to be Happy
43 I Love My Body (Men)
44 I Love My Body (Women)
45 How to Attract Love
46 Relationship Reprogramming
47 Freedom From Guilt
48 Get More Joy Out of Sex (Male)
49 Get More Joy Out of Sex (Female)
50 Freedom From Sexual Guilt
51 Freedom From Worry
52 Peace of Mind
53 My Parents. Myself
54 Loss of a Loved One
55 Handling Disappointment
56 Handling Divorce (Yes)
57 Handling Divorce (No)
58 How to Handle Children
59 Spice
60 Loneliness
61 Up From Depression
62 I Am Jealous
63 I Free You From Jealousy
64 Successful Retirement
65 Death and Dying
66 Stuttering
67 Touch Me
68 Hyperactive Children
69 Stop Being Angry

**SUCCESS SERIES**
70 Subconscious Sales Power
71 How to Make A Decision
72 Creative Thinking
73 Problem Solving
74 Goal Setting
75 Effective Speaking
76 Money-Prosperity
77 Self Confidence
78 Develop Enthusiasm
79 Fear of Success
80 Money-Compensation
81 Fear of Failure
82 Will Power
83 How to Be Popular

**PSYCHIC TAPE SERIES**
84 Develop Your Psychic Abilities
85 Past Life Regression
86 Astral Projection
87 Mind Projection
88 Chakra Meditation
89 Psychic Healing
90 Past Life Therapy
91 Talents/Abilities From Past Life
92 Visualization-Aura Reading
93 Past Life Regression with Present Mate/
94 Parallel Lives-Separate Selves      Lover
95 Birth Control
96 Conception
97 Spiritual-Psychic Protection

**SUBLIMINAL SUGGESTION SERIES**
98 Weight Loss
99 Better Memory
100 Prosperity
101 Enthusiasm
102 Tell Your Feeling How to Feel
103 Get More Joy Out of Sex (Male)
104 Get More Joy Out of Sex (Female)
105 Freedom From Worry
106 Creative Thinking
107 Self Confidence
108 Concentration
109 Good Study Habits
110 Control Drinking Habits
111 Lower Blood Pressure
112 How to Attract Love
113 Effective Speaking
114 Subconscious Sales Power
115 Freedom from Sexual Guilt

**SPORTS SERIES**
116 Be a Better Bowler
117 How to be a Great Golfer
118 Tennis
119 Baseball-Pitching
120 Baseball-Hitting
121 Baseball-Catching
122 Running

# ORDER FORM
## CIRCLE CORRESPONDING NUMBERS FROM LIST ABOVE -

| | | | | | | | | | | | | | | | | | | | | | | | | | | | | | | |
|---|---|---|---|---|---|---|---|---|---|---|---|---|---|---|---|---|---|---|---|---|---|---|---|---|---|---|---|---|---|---|
| 1 | 2 | 3 | 4 | 5 | 6 | 7 | 8 | 9 | 10 | 11 | 12 | 13 | 14 | 15 | 16 | 17 | 18 | 19 | 20 | 21 | 22 | 23 | 24 | 25 | 26 | 27 | 28 | 29 | 30 | 31 |
| 32 | 33 | 34 | 35 | 36 | 37 | 38 | 39 | 40 | 41 | 42 | 43 | 44 | 45 | 46 | 47 | 48 | 49 | 50 | 51 | 52 | 53 | 54 | 55 | 56 | 57 | 58 | 59 | 60 | | |
| 61 | 62 | 63 | 64 | 65 | 66 | 67 | 68 | 69 | 70 | 71 | 72 | 73 | 74 | 75 | 76 | 77 | 78 | 79 | 80 | 81 | 82 | 83 | 84 | 85 | 86 | 87 | 88 | 89 | | |
| 90 | 91 | 92 | 93 | 94 | 95 | 96 | 97 | 98 | 99 | 100 | 101 | 102 | 103 | 104 | 105 | 106 | 107 | 108 | 109 | 110 | 111 | 112 | 113 | 114 | | | | | | |
| 115 | 116 | 117 | 118 | 119 | 120 | 121 | 122 | | | | | | | | | | | | | | | | | | | | | | | |

Check: _____ Cassette, or 8-Track _____

● $9.98 per Tape    No. of Tapes _____    Subtotal **$** _____

☐ I've enclosed a check or money order **in the amount of:** _____

_____    _____
*Signature*                              *Date*

Name _____

Address _____ Apt. _____

City _____ Zip _____

State _____

**$2.00**
Shipping & Handling

**$** _____
6% Sales Tax CA Res.

**$** _____

**TOTAL**

**Mail your order to:   PARK WEST**
**P.O. Box 1502**
**Sausalito, CA 94965**